Creative Prescriptions™

for Women with Cancer

Tools for Tapping into
Your Stress-Free, Creative,
Happy Healing Space

By Annette Tello, M.S.

BALBOA
PRESS

A DIVISION OF HAY HOUSE

Balboa Press books may be ordered through booksellers or by contacting:

Balboa Press
A Division of Hay House
1663 Liberty Drive
Bloomington, IN 47403
www.balboapress.com
1 (877) 407-4847

ISBN: 978-1-9822-2912-2 (sc)
ISBN: 978-1-9822-3342-6 (e)

Library of Congress Control Number: 2019912040

Print information available on the last page.

Balboa Press rev. date: 08/30/2019

To Jim, the love of my life.
To my children, Jason and Monica.
To all the beautiful and courageous women diagnosed with cancer,
this is for you.

Contents

Acknowledgments

I would not have completed this book without the
generosity of the following amazing women.
Thank you to my daughter Monica, for your endless support
and feedback of the content and design of this book.
Thank you, Dr. Christina Horner, and Debra Melamed for your endorsements.
I would like to acknowledge Anja Polak-Mullins and Elizabeth Becker
for their time and invaluable feedback. Thank you for sharing your
insights and wisdom. This book is better for your suggestions.
A special thanks to Susanne Romo. I am grateful for all of your support and
editing skills, but most of all, I want to thank you for believing in me.

A special thanks to Juan Arteaga and the AP art students of Eastlake High School (2018) in Chula Vista, California, for the amazing drawings they contributed to the book. Thank you!

Artist Credits

Introduction

I developed the *Creative Prescriptions* program to specifically address many of the challenges faced by cancer patients. While you are in treatment, your medical team will take care of your body. However, you are more than your body; you are an intellectual, emotional, intuitive, spiritual, and creative being. All of these aspects of the self are affected by cancer, and should be included in the healing process. *Creative Prescriptions* helps you to tap into your inherent ability to be creative and its potential to heal physically, emotionally, psychologically, and spiritually. Creativity is your "prescription" to reduce stress, raise spirits, and gain a sense of control over your own healing.

This book is meant to be your companion through your treatment and recovery because it is a creative first-aid kit to use as needed. The best part is that no previous artistic skills are required. All you need is to trust yourself, and be willing to play and explore expressing yourself creatively.

Everyone's cancer journey is different. Use this guide to create your own unique and personal prescription to navigate your healing and recovery from cancer. Through this process, you will become not just a survivor but also a creative thriver.

Why Taking Time for Creative Expression Is Important during Cancer Treatment

Don't let cancer take all the joy and color out of your life!

As a cancer coach for women undergoing treatment I know that even if a woman is getting the best medical care, treating her "cancer" does not include the needs of the whole person. Creativity is a valuable personal resource to support your entire healing process. The tools that you will learn in this book are designed to help you use creativity to tap into your stress-free happy healing space. As you will learn from the research on creative expression, creativity literally helps you reduce stress and increase feelings of happiness, allowing your body to enter a relaxed healing state. You might ask; You get all this by playing with art supplies? Yes!

When you add creative expression to your treatment plan, you are empowering yourself to take an active role in your own healing process. Women who take responsibility, who "own" their health issues, feel empowered to make changes to conquer their cancer and live healthier lives. Being proactive in your emotional health reduces your feelings of fear and hopelessness. Healing through the creative arts may not result in being *cured* of a disease; however, it can lead to a feeling of *wholeness*, which is healing in and of itself.

In his book *Creative Healing*, Dr. Michael Samuels describes how art heals: "Our physiology changes from one of stress to one of relaxation, from one of fear to one of creativity and inspiration." In the *European Journal of Cancer Care* (January 2018), a review of fifteen studies on the art-making process for people with a cancer diagnosis stated, "Individual art-making can provide learning about [the] self, diversion and pleasure, self-management of pain, a sense of control, and enhanced social relationships."

Because of the extensive research documenting the many benefits of creative expression for cancer patients, many hospitals are offering art therapy classes. Unfortunately, not every hospital offers these classes, or they are not easy for patients to attend. Therefore, I wanted to create a flexible alternative to bring the healing benefits of the art-making/creative process to my clients in a way that was easy, enjoyable, therapeutic, and affordable.

I designed *Creative Prescriptions* for you to enjoy the benefits of the art-making process in the comfort of your own home, with a box of colored pencils. A caretaker can also implement the tools and activities to support a cancer patient, or the activities can be done in community support groups.

In the chapters that follow, we will investigate more of the research that supports the creative arts as a healing modality for cancer patients.

How This Book Came to Be

For the last twenty-five years, my work has focused on helping people with health issues or cancer, as a rehabilitation counselor, health coach, and cancer coach. In recent years, I worked for a non-profit agency, where I helped women navigate their cancer journey. What struck me was that these clients had many needs and challenges that were not being met by our program nor by other service providers in the community. One of the challenges was the lack of accessible tools to alleviate the emotionally overwhelming experience cancer patients and their families face in their daily lives.

I knew from personal experience that creative expression in the form of *art-making was an instrumental tool in my own healing from cervical carcinoma*. This inspired me to create a program that would give cancer patients creative tools to help them cope with their challenges and facilitate the healing process, in between doctors' appointments.

Creative Prescriptions allows for deep self-reflection and self-discovery without being analyzed or "fixed." It is about exploring the *process* of creating that allows us to tap into the healing benefits. Creative self-expression, in and of itself, is a coping tool that you will use throughout the book.

My Cancer Scare and the Power of Creative Healing

> *We can allow ourselves to be empowered, to induce self-healing through the creative aspects of poetry, music, art, and images and let them work within us to help cure our diseases and heal our lives.*
> —Bernie S Siegel, MD

Creativity can tap into a healing energy that is available to everyone. We tap into it when we are present and open during the creative process. In the *European Journal of Cancer Care* (January 2018), a review of fifteen studies on the art-making process for people with cancer used an adapted version of the Kaplan's Attention Restoration Theory (ART) to interpret the studies. The purpose of the study was to explore how art-making could help address the fatigue of cancer patients. The study states: "When viewed through the lens of ART, art-making can be understood as an energy-restoring activity that has the potential to enhance the lives of people with a diagnosis of cancer." This study confirms my personal experience that through my art-making I can tap into an energy that is profound, restorative, and energizing.

My Story

In my mid-thirties, I was a typical harried wife, mother, and working woman. I had a good life but inside I felt as though I was living the life that was expected of me. Then the bottom fell out when I was diagnosed and treated for cervical carcinoma in situ. I was lucky that it was caught early. However, my cancer diagnosis scared me to my core and prompted me to reevaluate my life and my priorities. I needed to make time to take better care of myself by doing things that nourished my body and soul.

During my teenage years art-making, kept me going through a difficult time in my life. I realized I had not done any art-making in years because I was "too busy." Therefore, I decided to take a botanical drawing class to help me reconnect to my creative self. During the first class the teacher told us to go outside and find a spot in the woods where we could find wildflowers and draw them. I was so excited that I would not be spending the whole class time inside on such a beautiful day. I grabbed my materials and went looking for some flowers to draw. I happily walked through the adjoining woods and picked out a quiet spot where I found little white flowers popping out through the leaves that had fallen the previous fall.

I sat down, took out my drawing pad, and studied the tiny leaves and petals of the flowers. I became completely present as I focused on drawing the details of the delicate flowers. Suddenly, I felt an energy that radiated from the top of my head and flooded into every cell of my body. I felt waves and waves of blissful energy wash over me, and when it was over, I felt a profound sense of peace, joy, and well-being. My body was vibrating with this amazing healing energy for several hours afterward.

My art-making process turned into a profound healing experience and the most amazing thing is that it only took about ten minutes!

This transformational moment filled me with blissful, loving energy that was healing to my body, mind, and soul. It felt as though I had been seeing the world in black and white and suddenly, I could see in vibrant color again. This motivated me to make lifestyle changes to improve my health and nurture my creative lifeline. I was on a creative journey to wellness.

Do not underestimate the healing power of creativity!

Shaun McNiff, art therapist and the author of *Art Can Heal Your Life*, feels that creating is all about energy. This element is frequently overlooked in the art-making experience. He describes the circulation of creative energy as a part of the art-making process, which provides healing energy to the body. It's important to be open to connecting to this energy without expectations that it will be a certain way. Of course, I do not always experience such intense energy every time I make art. However, I do experience subtle forms of energy moving through me as I create art, and I want you to know that these healing energies are available to you too, through the *Creative Prescriptions* tools and activities.

Overview

Creative Prescriptions is a guide for creating your own personal wellness program to support you during treatment. This guide allows you to bring all aspects of yourself into the healing process. *Creative Prescriptions* is not about mastering art techniques; it is about the *process* of "making art" as a form of intuitive self-expression that allows us to tap into its healing benefits.

Cancer patients can navigate their healing and recovery by selecting from six basic *prescriptions, that address specific challenges and offer corresponding creative coping tools.* Pick the prescription you need at the time and go right to that activity. For example, if you are "feeling fearful," chapter 5 has an activity to address this. Use this guide in the way it feels the best to you, your process and path are uniquely yours. The six *Creative Prescriptions* are:

1. Trust Your Intuition
2. Make Yourself a Priority
3. Express Yourself
4. Manage Your Mind-Set
5. Connect to Your Body's Wisdom
6. Cultivate a Spiritual Practice

You can personalize your process by using this book in three ways:

1. You can experience the tools and activities on an as-needed basis, as a creative first aid kit or as a form of self-care.
2. You can use this as a tool for experimentation, exploration, and personal growth. Personal growth occurs when there is a change, a shift, or a new insight as a result of an experience. To go deeper, we use:

   - *Creative expression/art-making* as a vehicle for exploring and experiencing the therapeutic benefits of the creative process.
   - *Journaling* as a vehicle for recording and integrating your experiences.

3. You can use a combination of the two processes.

Each section has different fonts so things are easy to find. The majority of the information is in the *Century Schoolbook* font.

- Activities are in Segoe Print
- Journal questions are in Courier New
- Client stories are in Bradley Hand

Unfortunately, I had to cut out a lot of information and activities from this book. I do not want you to miss out on the deleted information, so go to www.annettetello. com and sign up for bonus material!

What You Will Need to Get Started

This book is meant to be a portable art studio and journal. If you have not used art supplies in years, then start with a beginner's mind—be open, receptive, and curious. In addition, it's okay to get messy in this book!

We will go into details of art supplies in the next chapter. For now, all you need is some time—five to twenty minutes, depending on the activity—and a box of twelve or twenty-four colored pencils. Buy the best quality you can afford; I recommend Prismacolor. If you cannot get your hands on a box of colored pencils, just grab a pen and start with that.

If you have more supplies available, I recommend you make a portable art kit that you can carry in your purse, along with this book.

> Portable Art Kit
>
> Zippered pencil holder containing colored pencils, colored ink pens, eraser, pencil sharpener, glue stick, and child-safe scissors

In addition to creative expression, journaling is a major *Creative Prescriptions* tool that you will use throughout this book to help you explore your journey to well-being. If you do a lot of writing, there may not be enough space in this book, so you may want to buy an additional journal.

> *Journaling is a gift that you give to yourself to help you "stop" and take some time to reflect on what is going on in your life.*

This book is a safe place to express your thoughts, emotions, and creative soul. To get started on your creative journey to wellness, take some time to slow down, and enjoy coloring the following image.

CHAPTER 1

The Healing Power of Creativity

The creative journey has lasting and wide-spread therapeutic effects.
—Doreen Virtue, *The Courage to Be Creative*

How Creative Expression Can Help Us Heal

Artists know they can use their creativity to help them deal with life's challenges. The art-making process teaches us how to overcome fear and self-doubt. It allows us to practice stepping out of our comfort zone. Art-making teaches us to trust our intuitive promptings and be accepting of things when they don't work out the way we want them to. It helps us to transform emotional distress into creative works. In addition, art-making and creativity teaches us to let go, relax, and have fun *playing*. All these skills can help us through our healing process!

Creative expression gives you a new way of seeing and processing your illness—a way to expand your perspective about your situation. This program empowers you to tap into the healing benefits of creativity. The healing benefits do not necessarily mean that it will *cure* your cancer, but it can support a feeling of well-being, thus improving your day-to-day functioning and your quality of life. For the purposes of this book, "healing" is defined as *restoring your own personal sense of balance and well-being*.

Receiving a cancer diagnosis is likely one of the most devastating experiences of your life. Coping with the emotional free fall cancer brings is no easy task. It becomes easier, however, when you give yourself the room to express and honor what you are feeling. When I am with my clients, I give them a safe space to express themselves, to express the good, the bad, and the ugly. I want them to feel *heard* and *validated*. Since I cannot be with you, holding your hands across the kitchen table, I would like you to see this book as a safe place to express and honor your thoughts and feelings.

1

Instead of letting the roller coaster of emotions over run your life, you can channel those emotions to fuel your creativity. In this book, you will use creativity to explore what is troubling you, allowing for new ways of revealing and expressing your emotions and feelings. When your emotions are on the canvas, you can see them from a different perspective. You can gain fresh insight and wisdom. When you express emotions creatively, you can promote a state of relaxation that supports the body's natural ability to heal.

In her book *Release your Creativity*, Rebecca Schweitzer states, "The joy is in the mess, the glorious, the ugly, the mistakes, the success, and the feeling of how great it is to express yourself!"

This is what I want for you, my dear! I want you to express everything that you are feeling while you are going through recovery so when you complete your treatment, you are ready to move on. You will be ready to get on with your life as a stronger, wiser, more emotionally-healthy, and creative version of yourself.

While going through treatment, experiencing yourself as a creative person can help you see yourself in a more positive and life-affirming way. Creativity is in our DNA, and you don't have to be a master painter or a musician in order to express it, you just have to trust the process.

> *Not all of us are painters, but we are all artists.*
> —Sister Mary Corita Kent

Let's start exploring creativity and wellness with these journal questions:

Do I have tools to distract my mind, ease my pain, and soothe my soul while I am in treatment?

What do I give to myself on a regular basis that feels healing, creative, and nourishing?

Do I feel it would be beneficial to weave creativity into my daily activities?

Research on the Healing Benefits of Creativity

> *I have found that the drawings cancer patients create of their disease and its treatment reveal much about how they will respond to treatment. The drawings often uncover beliefs and attitudes that can positively or negatively affect healing.*
>
> —Bernie S. Siegel, MD

Many hospitals are now developing arts in medicine programs or art therapy programs because research has demonstrated that art-making and other forms of creative expression enhance the healing process. Studies show that "artistic skill" is not necessary to receive the therapeutic benefits of creative self-expression. What is more important is that you find a medium (coloring, painting, crafts) that you enjoy and make it a conscious form of self-care.

Hospitals use art therapy and creative activities to help patients cope with the symptoms of treatment and reduce the stress of illness. The Montreal Museum of Fine Arts is allowing physicians to write prescriptions for free museum visits for their patients. The museum supports the idea that "art is good medicine." In a 2017 report, the Parliamentary Group on Arts, Health and Wellbeing in the UK stated,

"The time has come to recognize the powerful contribution the arts can make to our health and well-being."

Creativity promotes healing of our minds and bodies by allowing us to unwind, releasing physical stress and anxiety, which is helpful when one is hospitalized or undergoing treatment. For cancer patients, creating something can give them a sense of empowerment when they are feeling overwhelmed and not in control of their situation. In his book *Creative Healing*, Dr. Michael Samuels describes how art heals:

1. Making art puts a person in a different brain wave pattern and affects the autonomic nervous system, hormonal balances, and brain neurotransmitters.
2. Making art affects every cell in the body instantly to create a healing physiology that changes the immune system and blood flow to the organs.
3. It changes attitudes, emotional states, and pain perception.

Creating art can reduce your pain. This is art as medicine! A study done at the Mayo Clinic in Rochester and published in the *European Journal of Cancer Care* showed that patients who participated in a brief bedside visual art intervention (BVAI) had "significant improvements in positive mood and [reduced] pain scores." In this study, BVAI allowed patients to create art without a "specific psychotherapeutic goal," meaning they could create whatever they wanted.

The good news is that you can receive the healing benefits of creative expression in the comfort of your own home. A study in the *Journal of Health Psychology* (2006), by researchers Collie, Bottorff, and Long, titled "A Narrative View of Art Therapy and Art-Making by Women with Breast Cancer", stated, "There is wide clinical acceptance of the value of art therapy and therapeutic art-making in cancer care." The researchers found that participants experienced the therapeutic benefits of the art-making process whether they were in an art therapy group or made art on their own.

Art Therapy versus Creative Expression

In art therapy, the goal is to use the arts for diagnosis and treatment within a therapeutic relationship with a licensed therapist. This book is not art therapy and is not meant to replace professional help for those who have a history of mental health issues, clinical depression, trauma, or abuse. If you are struggling with this, please seek professional help.

Even though *Creative Prescriptions* is not art therapy, you can still benefit from the therapeutic benefits of creative expression offered in this book. This book is about the process of using creativity to express thoughts and release emotions. Once the thoughts and emotions are *seen* through the creative process, it can lead to *understanding* and *resolving*.

This process is similar to expressive arts therapy in that the focus is on the process of creation. According to Wikipedia, expressive arts therapy is defined as follows: "Unlike traditional art expression, the process of creation is emphasized rather than the final product. Expressive therapy is predicated on the assumption that people can heal through use of imagination and the various forms of creative expression."

In expressive arts, drama, dance movements, music, and poetry/writing are commonly used in addition to the visual arts. Most of this work is done in hospitals or health care facilities, which is another reason for the creation of this book. I want these tools to be available to everyone, not just for patients in hospitals or in clinical therapy.

Why Does Society Minimize the Importance of Our Creativity?

Some people feel art is frivolous, indulgent, and a waste of time. Don't let others stop you from using your creativity and self-expression for well-being! Most people do not know about the healing benefits of the arts, so they may not understand why you are spending your time doing this. Explain to your family why it is important to you, and if they still do not understand, it is okay to have this one thing just for yourself without having to justify it. You are entitled to some creative "me time." If you are struggling with justifying giving yourself some time, let's start with exploring your thoughts regarding your time and creativity.

Journal Questions:

What is stopping me from giving myself the time and space to be creative?

Are these reasons worth limiting my creativity and it's healing benefits?

Where in my life can I find some time for myself and my creativity? Can I give up thirty minutes of surfing the Internet, social media, or watching television?

Taking Time for Yourself

Creative self-expression gives your deepest and wisest self the time and space to speak to you.

Many of my clients tell me "I don't have the time to make art!" I understand that concern. Yes, making-art takes a little bit of time, but what's wrong with that? What would you rather be doing? The laundry? Watching another sitcom rerun? I think many women feel that to be creative, you must have a lot of space, time, and money (for expensive art supplies). However, you need very little of these things, just a kitchen table, a little bit of time (five to fifteen minutes), and some colored pencils. That's it! That is all you really need to express your creativity in this book.

I get up early just to allow myself time for art; sometimes it's only 15 minutes, but it totally changes the course of my day just by spending a little time in my happy place.

—Tiffany Goff Smith, journal artist

Would it help if you thought of your "creative" time as "self-care" time? Time is one of the most precious gifts you can give yourself. The time you give to yourself is one of the few things you have *complete control* over! You just need to decide you're worth it. I treat my creativity as a relationship that I set some time aside to cultivate and nurture. I find that my creative time is my happy time. What creativity gives to me more than makes up for the time spent.

This book is designed so you can take it to your medical appointments. You can use your waiting room time as self-care time. While waiting for treatment you can nurture your creativity instead of worrying.

As adults, it is important that we let our families know that the process of creating, or "making art," is essential to our well-being and for them to respect this process. I created a Do Not Disturb sign for you to use. Hang it on your doorknob when you need some creative "me time." In the next chapter we will spend some time exploring and reclaiming our creativity.

Activity: "Do Not Disturb" Door Hanger

Enjoy coloring the door hanger. Cut it out when completed and use as needed.

CHAPTER 2

Reclaiming Your Creativity

There is so much potential and so much beauty and transformation that is to be found inside our own creative voices. The only way to liberate it is to use it.

—Melissa Dinwidde, artist

Where to Start

You do not have to be a professional chef to create a wonderful dinner. Likewise, you do not have to be an artist to make art or express yourself creatively. The truth is that we are all creative, although we may not express it by painting a beautiful landscape.

If someone tells you they can't read or write, you don't assume they are not capable of it, just that they haven't learned how. It's the same with creativity.

—Ken Robinson, *Out of Our Minds: The Power of Being Creative*

Reclaiming your creativity starts with *trusting* yourself, trusting what needs to be expressed through experimenting and exploring with open curiosity. The most important thing to remember is that you do not need any special training or drawing classes to benefit from the art-making process. Don't let cultural definitions of what an "artist" is keep you from the healing and uplifting benefits of making art.

The activities in this book will allow us to slip into our creativity by taking the time to just play, explore, and experiment with different ways of expressing ourselves! This process, or *way* of being creative, allows us to relax our critical minds and slip into the creative parts of our brains. This is how we can tap into our creativity and our unique voices. The process will be healing because it will be spontaneous expression; it will be what you need in that moment, whether it is a release of pent-up emotions or the joy of playing with art materials.

Product versus Process

In art school, I had to *produce* artwork for grades, and frankly, it's hard work! The final "product" was a carefully planned concept that included rough drafts, composition, perspective, a color study, and a mastery of technique. I never enjoyed producing this type of art. I find that art that expresses *emotions* is more interesting than art that shows a well-executed plan. Expressive works of art feel more mysterious, exciting, meaningful, and alive. I want you to experience the joy and the sense of aliveness that comes when you express yourself in this spontaneous way, but before we do, let's explore your beliefs about creativity in the following questions.

Journal Questions:

What are my beliefs about my ability to be creative?

What am I longing to express?

Creativity takes many forms—cooking, gardening, crafting, and so on. What is my favorite way of being creative?

To Share or Not to Share Your Artwork

In the beginning, I recommend that you keep your creative images private. You are just beginning to explore and trust your unique way of expressing yourself, and you need time to grow into this new aspect of yourself. However, studies show that making art in complete isolation can increase the feelings of isolation. Therefore, once you feel ready, I encourage you to share your work with a therapist, a support group, or with a loved one who supports your creative expression.

An art therapy group or a support group is a great place to share your work. Groups have guidelines that include honoring everyone's privacy and respecting other people's creations. Art therapy groups usually have a "no comment on other people's work" rule, which is a necessary boundary.

When we feel safe in being open and vulnerable with others, we are taking steps in our lives to be more open and authentic with ourselves. In this type of setting, creating art that expresses deep emotions, then sharing your art and being heard, can be healing. Sometimes our creativity works in mysterious ways, and you may find that your creations will be beneficial and healing to your viewers.

Creating art with others, such as in an art therapy group or art class, brings a creative energy that you may not feel when working alone. There are also benefits in sharing your artwork in a nontherapeutic setting because you can receive some feedback that might open your perception. This may deepen your experience. However, use discernment and only share your artwork with people who have earned the right to see and comment on your work.

For those of you who would like to share your artwork on a safe and supportive online site, join my Facebook group: Fb.me/creativeprescriptions

Supplies

> *Artistic expression, even through the humblest materials, is a way of experiencing and knowing spirit.*
> —Cathy Malchiodi, *The Soul's Palette*

Work with What You Have

I encourage you to work with what you have. If you only have a blue pen, you can start with that. It's the *process* of creating that brings us the healing benefits, not the materials. However, creative mediums have different traits, and just like people, you may prefer one medium over another.

Don't think limited art supplies will limit your ability to be creative! A study from the University of Illinois suggests that scarcity of materials enhances creativity. This is true! I got my reputation as being the most creative kid in my classrooms by not having the right art supplies, or enough supplies, and having to come up with unique and unusual ways to complete my assignments. This taught me how to think "outside the box," which ultimately led to the creation of this book.

Optional Art Supplies

In this book, we are mostly going to be using colored pencils because they are the easiest to use in this format. However, feel free to substitute materials listed for the activities with other mediums. I recommend you purchase a *mixed media art journal* if you want to use a variety of media to do the activities. *There is no right or wrong way to do it.* Everyone is different, so feel free to do a little exploring to find out what works for you.

In addition to using colored pens and pencils, you can experiment with the following:

Drawing: Markers, pastels, gel pens, inks, and crayons.
Paint: Watercolor and acrylic paint and watercolor pencils. If you use acrylics, consider using matte paint because it is easier to write over.

In selecting new art supplies, pick a medium that you are drawn to. Go to an arts and crafts store and walk around to see what sparks your interest. Gathering art supplies is a reason to get excited and gives you something to look forward to, a new thing to play with. If you are not up for a shopping trip, order supplies online. If you have children, raid their art supplies.

Your "Studio"

> *The studio, whether a room or a drawing journal, can be an oasis from stress, an emotional refuge, a source of wisdom, or a place of spiritual renewal.*
>
> —Cathy Malchiodi, *The Soul's Palette*

Your studio can be between the covers of this book; it can be a whole room; it can be the kitchen table or outside under a tree. Wherever you decide to create, consider that space to be your sacred creative space. When you create from this space, you can tap into a more intuitive way of expressing yourself. *Use what you have.*

Your Inner Critic

Teacher and artist Howard Ikemoto tells a story about his daughter, who was seven years old when she asked him what he did at work. He told her his job at the college was to teach people how to draw. She gave him an incredulous look and said, "You mean they forgot?"

Many of us have forgotten that as children we could pick up a paintbrush and start painting without any hesitation. What happened to that fearless creativity? While in grade school, most of us enjoyed our creativity without the inner and outer critics. We were spontaneous and enjoyed expressing ourselves from our creative souls. Somewhere along the line, we became self-conscious as we were exposed to criticism of our art. In school we learned to minimize the value of art, making it trivial, not as important as math or science.

> *Every child is an artist. The problem is how to remain an artist once we grow up.*
>
> —Pablo Picasso

Growing up, those of us that were criticized about our creations, internalized this to form our "inner critic." We believed the inner critic that told us we were not artists, so we stopped creating. Sometimes it's the people currently in our lives who look down on our "little hobby," and think it's a waste of our time.

Even though I did receive many positive affirmations growing up that I was "a good artist," I also had an art teacher tell me that *I had no talent, that I was not creative.* Fortunately for me, art-making was not about talent; it was about expressing my soul from a place of authenticity and freedom. It was about respecting myself and honoring my unique creative voice. My hope, dear one, is that you can adopt this same attitude toward your creativity and art-making process.

We are all creative, even if we may not fit into an art teacher's ideas of what a certain subject should look like. Some people think they are not good at art because they are unable to replicate an image they have in their mind. All artists, even professional artists, struggle with this dilemma! Don't let that stop you from enjoying the benefits of this book.

Sometimes the problem is that we are our own worst critic! Judgment is the number one killer of creativity. If you are judging your painting and thinking, *This is ugly!* ask yourself, *Can I make it uglier?* This is a great way to free yourself from the inner critic and unleash your creative soul! Understand that these "ugly" paintings are the seeds of your self-expression that need time and space to sprout. Give them the chance to bloom into your full unique voice. The following questions will help you explore your inner critic.

Journal Questions:

How old was I when I received my first criticism of my artwork? What happened? How did it make me feel?

How did it affect my creativity?

How does it affect me now?

Silencing the Inner Critic

If you hear a voice within you saying "You are not a painter," then by all means paint, and that voice will be silenced.

—Vincent van Gogh

There are two keys to silencing the "inner critic." The first key is *practicing* at being creative, for when you are practicing, you don't expect to be good at it, so your inner critic will not have much to say. You practice from a place of curiosity asking, "What if?" *What if I draw blue dots over the whole drawing?* This leads you to being open to experimentation and exploration.

The second key is to just start—start *playing* with art materials without any expectations on how it has to look. Having fun drawing, painting, and writing, without judgment, is a soothing balm over any art wounds.

It's not always easy to keep our spirits up when going through the stress of treatment and the accompanying side effects, so it's important to have activities we can trust to help us feel better. Let the *Creative Prescriptions* activities help you tap into the carefree creativity you experienced as a child. Playing with art supplies helps you to get in touch with the enjoyment found in the present moment, allowing you to forget about your worries and problems.

Making art can be a playful way to tune into your intuition, listen to your heart, and gain clarity in your life. This chapter includes creative warm-ups to help you start. If you did not get to play with art materials as a child, then it is not too late to start!

Activity: Creative Play

What kinds of creativity did you enjoy as a child? Coloring/painting? Cutting and pasting? Building things? Playing with clay?

Why did you enjoy these activities?
Can you do a variation of the things you enjoyed, now?

As a child, I remember spending hours playing with paper dolls. Enjoy coloring the following paper doll and the cute clothing.

Boosting Your Creativity

You can't use up creativity. The more you use it the more you have.
—Maya Angelou

The purpose of the simple activities that we will do in this section is to help us connect to that joyful place we used to create from as children. This will allow you to begin building your confidence and trusting your intuitive promptings, opening the door to *trusting your unique voice.* Consider setting some time aside during the week when you can focus on one creative activity at a time.

I found I could say things with color and shapes that I couldn't say any other way—things I had no words for.
—Georgia O'Keeffe

Creativity is not something that is learned; it is something that we all have. We just need to get out of our own way and give it a bit of time to come out and play. Studies have shown that having the ability to creatively *express yourself* can lead to increased feelings of well-being, self-empowerment, and self-esteem. I know I have experienced all of these feelings through my art-making!

The Building Blocks of Art

Art is a line around your thoughts.
—Gustav Klimt

The basic building blocks of art include line, shape, texture, and color. You can express yourself with these simple tools. Everyone can draw a line (it does not need to be perfectly straight), make a shape, and color it in with colored pencils or other mediums. You can create texture by making smaller marks in a pattern. Let's start with something as simple as tracing your hand, drawing some random lines and shapes, and then coloring it in.

Activity: Creative Hand

Complete the following hand by adding more lines and shapes, then color it in.

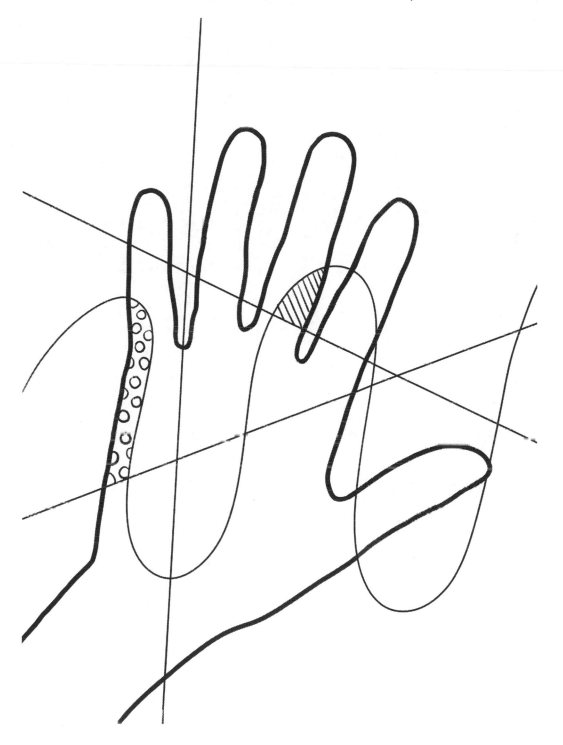

Activity: Playing with Art Supplies

Find ways throughout the week that you can play with art supplies for ten to fifteen minutes. Experiment by playing with the art supplies you currently have. On the following pages, play with different mediums and see how they interact with each other. Use stencils and stamps to create different textures. Ask yourself, *What if?* Play with the different mediums and find the one you enjoy the most. When you are done, answer the journal questions that follow.

Journal Questions:

What medium did I enjoy using the most?

Why did I like it?

What creative people do I admire? What mediums do they use?

Color Connection

The chief function of color should be to serve expression.
—Henri Matisse

In creative projects, we use color to express our emotions. Color can convey emotions in a way the written word cannot. Color is amazing because it can contribute to our well-being by lifting our spirits and can therefore affect our energy levels. The colors you encounter throughout your day can affect you in subtle ways, whether you are aware of it or not, so why not use color consciously?

The best color in the whole world is the one that looks good on you.
—Coco Chanel

We all have individual associations with colors, based on our personal experiences. Therefore, when you read a description of what a certain color means, it may or may not have the same meaning for you. For example, for some people, the color red represents anger, while other people feel that red represents love. To benefit from the language of color, it helps to understand your personal associations with different colors. Understanding how color affects your emotions will make you more confident in using it to express your feelings in the activities in this book.

For example, the primary color yellow feels happy and bright to me; however, if I make a drawing and use mustard yellow, that represents sadness to me. Color therapy goes into detail on how colors affect us, but how you experience color is ultimately personal. Understand that you may never fully know the meaning of every color that you use in your creations—and that's okay too.

Your mood is affected by your surroundings, so if you are not feeling well, it's important to surround yourself with the colors that make you feel good. You can use color to lift your spirits when you are feeling down or calm yourself when anxious. You can create an environment in your home that makes you feel nurtured, calm, and uplifted with the use of certain colors. Let's explore how you feel about color in the following questions.

Journal Questions:

What are my favorite colors?

Why do I like these colors? Are there memories attached to these colors?

What colors don't I like, and why?

Activity: Surround Yourself in Color

Supplies: Magazines for images, scissors, and glue stick

How can you surround yourself with your favorite colors? Cut out magazine images of clothing, accessories, bedding, furniture and so forth, in your favorite colors and paste them onto the blank page. Around the images, describe how the colors make you feel. Afterward, find ways to surround yourself with your favorite color, such as wrapping yourself in a scarf or soft sweater in a color that makes you happy.

CHAPTER 3

Creative Prescription 1: Trust Your Intuition

Trust yourself. You know more than you think.
                                        —Dr. Benjamin Spock

The Importance of Trusting Yourself and Your Medical Team

As a cancer and health coach working with people in treatment, I realized that those clients who trust themselves and their decisions concerning health do much better than those who defer to an outside source to make their decisions. Of course, you want all the medical facts and recommendations from your medical team, but your decisions must *feel right* to you too.

> *Trust is a reflection of the health and wealth of our relationship with ourselves.*
>
> —Natalie Lue

Having cancer is scary; therefore, when making treatment decisions, it is important to make your decisions from a state of trust versus a fear-based state. When you trust yourself, you can wholeheartedly say *yes* to your treatment because you believe in your decision and that will increase your feelings of confidence and hope. When you say yes from a place of *doubt*, you carry the energy of resistance and fear. This will cause feelings of anxiety and constant worrying and that does not lead to the best conditions for your healing.

> *If you are not listening to your ideas of what should happen ... and if you're not to trust your personal preferences or interpretations, what is left? What do you listen to?*
>
> —Michelle Cassou and Stewart Cubley
> *Life, Paint and Passion*

When you make decisions from a space of self-trust, you will minimize regrets. I have seen the results of clients who regret medical decisions, and it is so devastating to their emotional well-being. Studies have shown that patients who have a strong trust in their medical team and treatment have much better results, with fewer side effects. When we take the time to go inward, we can tap into what *feels right* in that situation. If you believe chemotherapy is the right choice for you, believe in it one hundred percent and go forward with confidence; this is the ticket to a smooth recovery.

The following client story illustrates why it's important to trust yourself during treatment:

Client Story

I went to visit one of my clients, and I found her in tears. She was upset that her doctor recommended a mastectomy and reconstruction of her left breast, when she thought she was going to have a lumpectomy for her stage 1 breast cancer. She was devastated by this news. She told me she knew this was not the right course of action for her, and she had fallen into a depression after hearing his treatment plan. I recommended she have a second opinion to determine if she had other options. She did see a second surgeon. He reviewed her medical records and diagnostic imaging, and he felt a lumpectomy was a viable choice. The client went back to the first doctor with the second opinion, and he agreed to do a lumpectomy. He did a beautiful job. After the surgery, she was happy with the results, but more important she was happy that she had trusted herself and did not give up on what she thought was the right choice for her.

I want all of my clients to be happy with their medical decisions. Trusting yourself increases confidence in your decisions which leads to emotional and mental fortitude. If there are side effects or complications to treatment, they are much easier to handle. During any discussions with your doctor about treatment, check in with yourself, constantly asking yourself, *Does this feel right to me?* If *yes*, go forward. If *no*, ask your doctor for clarification and if needed, some time to do research and think about your options. Unless it is an emergency, it is better not to rush into any medical decisions, especially if you are emotionally distraught.

Remember that you have the right to have all your questions answered; you have a right to have medical terminology explained to you, and you have a right to a second opinion to explore other options. If you are not comfortable with your doctor, tell your provider and ask to see another doctor. Don't worry about hurting the doctor's feelings—your peace of mind is more important!

Sometimes we realize that our logical minds can only take us so far; therefore, it is helpful to be open to other ways of obtaining information. For example, to make the best decisions for your medical treatment, use more than one form of knowing to inform your decision. In addition to the advice of your medical team, add medical research, your intuition, social input (from family and other cancer patients), and spiritual guidance to help you make the best choices for you and your family.

Journal Questions:

Am I making medical decisions from a place of confidence and self-trust?

If no, what can I do to increase self-trust?

Do I trust my Doctor completely?

If not, what can I do to improve this situation?

Creativity and Medicine

> *If you ever have an intuitive inner knowing, don't accept anyone else's opinion, pursue yours.*
>
> —Bernie S. Siegel, MD

When Dr. Bernie Siegel was practicing medicine, he had his patients use art to express how they felt about treatment or surgery. Dr. Siegel would ask his patients to do a simple drawing to answer two questions: "What do you think about your illness?" and "What do you think about treatment?" He would look at the drawings to help him and his patients understand how they felt about themselves and the medical interventions. He said, "I have found that the drawings cancer patients create of their disease and its treatment reveal much about how they will respond to treatment. The drawings often uncover beliefs and attitudes that can positively or negatively affect healing."

In a study about *art therapy* and *art-making* published in the *Journal of Health Psychology* (2006), by researchers Collie, Bottorff, and Long, their findings supported the theory that the *art-making* process gives you the ability to heal yourself. A cancer participant in the study stated, "It opens that pathway that allows you to use additional channels with which to heal yourself."

In the study, they discuss a participant who had a second diagnosis of breast cancer who had promised herself she would never go through chemotherapy again. However, after participating in an art therapy session, "she was surprised at what her drawings revealed." She stated, "I never imagined that that amount of information would come out of a small drawing that's on paper ... I was given insight that I wasn't aware of, which gave me a sense of empowerment, and then I was able to make the decision that I wanted from that."

After that session, she *knew* going back to chemotherapy was her best avenue for getting better. Wouldn't it be nice to make decisions from an empowering sense of knowing? In this chapter, we will explore *intuitive collage* as a tool to help us tap into our knowing, but first we will explore different types of intuition.

Exploring Different Types of Intuition

To understand how creativity can be used as a tool for healing, we are going to explore the intuitive aspects of art-making. In his book *Deep Medicine*, William B. Stewart, MD, states, "Any activity that helps us connect to our inner selves is health enhancing." He describes four practices that are common in many cultures for accessing the inner self (intuition): *slowing down, getting quiet, paying attention, and going inward.* We are going to use a variation of these practices in the activities that follow, but before we do, let's explore what intuition is.

What is intuition? On dictionary.com intuition is defined as:

1. a thing that one knows or considers likely from instinctive feeling rather than conscious reasoning.
2. the ability to understand something immediately, without the need for conscious reasoning.

Base on the above definitions there are two types of intuition. The most common type of intuition comes from an *instinctive* feeling that could be in the form of a body sensation, like a gut feeling. This is not woo-woo new age stuff! Being in tune with your body sensations helps your healing process because you are connected to the enteric nervous system, which contains neurotransmitters and is a part of the autonomic nervous system. Medical science calls this area the "second brain" because it has its own intelligence. When we have a "gut" feeling it is coming from the enteric system. The heart area also has a high level of neurotransmitters that can inform the body and mind. We have all heard the phrase "My heart tells me to …" or "My heart feels heavy when I think about..." *Your body has this ancient system to give you information to support your health and survival, so use it to help guide you throughout your treatment and recovery.*

To tap into this wisdom, ask yourself, *When thinking about an option, does my heart and body expand and feel light or does it feel contracted, tight, or heavy?* For me, expansion feels like a *yes* and contraction is a *no*. What does a *yes* feel like to you? What does a *no* feel like to you? There is a difference between what you *think* you should do and what you *feel* you should do. If your mind says *yes* but your body says *no*, you are out of alignment with your intuition and further exploration is needed.

The second type of intuition, when you understand things without "conscious reasoning," is called many things: inner knowing, inner wisdom, divine self, messages from the interior. Others call it their emotional guidance system or being in alignment with their higher self. Whatever you choose to call it, trusting your inner knowing is health enhancing.

Tapping into this type of *knowing* is an awareness that does not come from the logical brain. The information is clear on what you should do. You may hear a word, or see images, or you just *know*. If you are not sure if your thought is a cognitive thought or intuitive knowing, bring the thought down into your body and notice how it feels. Does it feel right, light, and expansive? Or is there still some heaviness and doubt?

Learning to listen and trust our intuition is a gift we can give ourselves to promote our health and well-being. When we trust our "knowing," we can let go of the need to control things because control is a fear-based mind-set. As women, we need to give ourselves the time and safe space to access our own wisdom, so let's take a little time to explore our intuition in the following questions.

Journal Questions:

How does my intuition communicate with me? In what part of my body do I normally feel my intuition?

When using gut instincts, what feels like a **yes** and what feels like a **no**?

Do I feel my intuition could be a valuable tool in making decisions regarding my health? Going forward in my treatment, how can I increase my trust in my intuition?

Creative Prescriptions Tools and Activities

This section covers *Creative Prescriptions* tools, activities, and journal questions, to explore and increase your connection to your intuitive knowing.

When You Want to Tap into Your Intuition through Creativity

> *Art-making is a great way of cracking the code of intuitive knowing. Think of pencils, crayons, clay, and collage as the technology of intuitive knowing and your imagination as the fuel that feeds this technology.*
> —Cathy A. Malchiodi, *The Soul's Palette*

Creative self-expression is a wonderful tool for connecting to our intuitive voice. When using creativity to tap into our intuition, we tune into subtle creative impulses. If we can learn to stay *present* with the subtle impulses, we can tap into our wisdom. This process is called *intuitive art* or *spontaneous expression*. This personal and spontaneous way to create is what helps you to connect to your body and your intuition.

You can use your creativity to tap into your intuition by doing the following:

1. Focus on what is in front of you.
2. Tune into your breath and your body.
3. Become present to subtle impulses as you start the activity.
4. Let what longs to be expressed come out through the art-making process.

This creative process helps you to connect with your intuition because the paper or canvas holds a space for you to be present, allowing you to tap into your subconscious or intuitive mind to receive its messages. During intuitive drawing or painting, you can stand in front of a big white canvas and not be afraid that you do not have a plan. You learn how to trust yourself from one *mark-making* decision to another. At its most basic level art-making is about *making-marks* with a pencil or paintbrush. When you create art in this way, you express what is internal and move it to the external (visual), where you can see it in a new light and from a different part of the brain, revealing new insights.

> *I art journal to see what wants to come out on the page from my subconscious ...*
> —Cheryl Sosnowski, journal artist

Many intuitive insights may come to you through art-making, collaging, art journaling, and other types of spontaneous expression. Do you know how freeing it is to be able to give yourself the time and space to express what your body and soul are longing to say? You can experience that in the next activity.

Collaging As an Intuitive Tool

Collage is a powerful tool that can help us connect to our authentic voice and intuition. Think of collaging as a process for gathering images that speak to your soul. The best thing about this technique is that you do not need "artistic skills" to make a meaningful collage. *Collage* comes from a French word that means "to glue," because one adheres images to a sheet of paper or canvas. It was a technique used by artist Marcel Mariën in the 1950s because initially he could not draw or paint. Collages mostly use images from magazines, but you can use anything that speaks to you. You can add paint, words, and other materials to the images. This is a great way to repurpose found materials like old photos and ephemera.

> *By paying attention to our physical self through collage and journaling, we allow the body to have a voice.*
>
> —Lucia Capacchione

Intuitive or spontaneous collage is about staying connected to the images and the energy that you are feeling in that moment. Your intuition speaks to you through, body sensations, feelings, images, colors, symbols and words. Collaging allows you to connect to the whisperings of your body/mind and realize the answers are not "out there"; they are inside of you.

This tool is easy and fun, but do not underestimate the ability of collaging to be emotionally revealing and healing. When collaging, set your intention on a question you need more information on or be open to any messages your body (subconscious mind) has for you. This will open you up to guidance and insight from your inner wisdom.

How to Collage

Collaging involves sitting down with a pile of magazines and tearing or cutting out images, words, and colors that capture your attention. When collaging, don't think too much about what you are selecting; this engages the "left" side of your brain, which is focused on logic and judgment. Try to stay in your "right" mind and body, focusing on things that move you, excite you, and draw you in with color and texture, based on the intention for the collage. Some therapists feel that the collage should only contain images and that words can be added afterward because "words" keep you in your logical left brain. Do what feels right for you.

When you feel you have enough images, arrange them on the page in a pleasing manner and then glue them in this book or in a journal. Afterward, look at the images. See if there is a pattern or a theme and ask yourself, *What are the images telling me?* In the next section I included a process to help you go deeper.

Activity: Intuitive Collage

To do this type of collage, allow for one to two uninterrupted hours. I recommend that you put on some relaxing music and have a cup of your favorite tea nearby. Use this time to let your intuition/body speak to you so you can honor your own inner wisdom. When you are doing this activity, do not rush or control the process; rather, surrender to this creative experience. This will allow for the most spontaneity and insights to come to you.

Supplies: scissors, glue stick, and a pile of magazines

Optional: markers, colored pencils, or paint

1. **Set the intention** to explore a specific question or be open to any messages that come to you. Take a deep breath and close your eyes, taking a moment to connect to your inner guidance by letting all other thoughts fall away. Just be still and present in your body. When you are centered, open your eyes.
2. **Select images** from magazines. Tear or cut out images that you are drawn to. Do not analyze why you are drawn to certain images. Cut these out, set them aside, and continue cutting out images that speak to you on a nonverbal level. Stop when you feel you have enough.
3. **Sort through the images** and select the ones that feel "right" for use. After you have done this, look at the images and see if any patterns emerge.
4. **Arrange the images** on the page in a way that is pleasing to you. When you are done, step back and look at your collage.
5. **Take some time to journal** about your experience and insights from this activity, by answering the questions that follow.

Journal Questions:

What were the main images or themes of my collage? Did the images surprise me?

What is my intuition/body telling me I need right now?

Do I feel this will be a helpful tool for me?

When You Want to Understand Your Images

> *When words are not enough, we turn to images and symbols to tell our stories. And in telling our stories through art, we find pathways to wellness, recovery and transformation.*
> —Cathy Malchiodi *The Soul's Palette*

Through art-making, you may receive images or symbols you don't understand. You may be tempted to search the Internet to find out what they mean, but I encourage you to be comfortable sitting with the unknown. Sometimes the "healing" comes from the emotional release of the process and nothing else is needed. Other times our intuition is expressing something deeper and speaks to us using images and symbols; to understand the meanings, we need to learn its secret language. Instead of analyzing the image, we can understand it by giving it a voice. We move from "What I *think* the image is about" to being in a state of openness about what the image has to convey to us.

When we give the image a voice, we move the discussion from the head into the heart and body. This means giving your image its own voice or personality. This is sometimes called *personification.* This is similar to poets giving flowers and the wind a voice. For now, know that you can access a different perspective with this technique.

Activity: Voice of the Image

After completing any visual art, hold the paper in front of your body with the image facing outward. You can "imagine" what the image would say if it could talk.

> Start by saying the following things from the voice of the image
>
> I am the image that is ready to speak to you.
>
> I am ...
>
> I want you to know ...
>
> I don't like that ...
>
> I want you to ...
>
> Then ask questions that you have of the image
>
> Write down what the image says to you and then answer the following journal questions.

Journal Questions:

How was this experience of "dialoging" with my art?

What did I discover about myself?

Was I able to experience a new way to connect to my heart, body, and intuition?

CHAPTER 4

Creative Prescription 2: Make Yourself a Priority

May your choices reflect your hopes, not your fears.
—Nelson Mandela

Choice Theory

Choice theory, developed by William Glasser, states, "People subconsciously choose to feel helpless, depressed, or stuck in old thought patterns and habits." He adds, "It is easier for people to continue doing what is comfortable … rather than making a choice to change these behaviors"—and that not doing anything is in fact a choice to "do nothing."

When cancer causes suffering, we can let the pain define us and take over our lives or we can use the pain as fuel to "choose" differently. We can use the pain to change things in our lives that no longer serve us. If it is something that we cannot change, we have a choice to accept it, or not accept it and prolong our suffering.

Pain is inevitable, suffering is a choice.
—Buddha

There is a difference between saying "I have to" versus "I choose to." When we act from our "choice," we feel nurtured by our decisions, but when we act from a space of "I have to," we see this as a sacrifice, and therefore it can depress our spirits and drain our energy. During cancer treatment, there are going to be many things that you "have to do"; therefore, when it deals with medical treatment, it helps to see treatment as a choice. For example, instead of saying "I have to have chemotherapy" say "I choose to have chemotherapy because it's the best option for me." This comes from a place of empowerment—that you are *choosing* to accept the treatment.

We make thousands of choices every day. Most of these choices are made from habit and are often not a *conscious* decision. With each choice you make every day, you are creating your unique and authentic life. In each situation you face and with every decision you make, your choices contribute to your illness or to your well-being. The small positive changes you make today will lead to your well-being in the future.

Client Story

A coaching client wanted to eat healthier but hated cooking because she saw it as a chore that she had to do. We worked on changing her mind-set by re-framing her belief. Once she saw that cooking for herself and her family was essential to good health, she "chose" to make cooking a more enjoyable experience. She made cooking more fun by taking cooking classes with her family. They created a cookbook with everyone's favorite recipes. Now the whole family works together in making the family meals. She really enjoys cooking now; it's a way to love and nurture her family and herself.

What is the ultimate secret to living a more creative, balanced, joyful, and healthier life? *You!* You have the power over all the areas of your well-being by reconnecting to your power of conscious choice. It is empowering to know that you have a choice, so be aware of the language or messages you say to yourself; make them affirming and empowering to you. In the following questions, you will journal about the choices you have been making about your health and the choices you will make this day forward that are more empowering and lead to your well-being.

Journal Questions:

What choices am I making that are robbing me of my health or are no longer working for me?

What can I let go of?

How can I reframe the things I "have to do," regarding my treatment, into a more positive message for myself?

It is Time to Make Yourself a Priority

When we focus our energy on everyone else's needs, it distracts us from connecting to our own dreams, desires, and needs.

If you have cancer, it is time to make yourself a priority! As women, many of us were raised to believe our self-worth comes from taking care of others and putting their needs before ours. Taking time for yourself is not *selfish*. Depleting your energy is not serving anyone, especially yourself. If you have received the diagnosis of cancer, it is time to put yourself first! It is time to treat yourself like an honored guest in your own life. When you treat yourself with love and care, you show others how to treat you.

While going through treatment, schedule some "me time" for yourself on a weekly basis. If you have time to watch a half hour of TV or surf the Internet, then you have half an hour to take some "me time." Time is the most precious gift you can give yourself right now, and using that time for creativity is a great way to self-nurture and self-care.

Learning to put yourself and your body first is essential for healing and wellness. When you give yourself time to take care of your needs, your positive actions trigger the release of hormones that support your healing process. Taking care of your needs is an act of self-love, and your body responds accordingly. If you think you are too busy to spend five to twenty minutes for self-care or creativity, then ask yourself the following questions.

Journal Questions:

Do I feel guilty for taking time for myself? Why?

What is more important than my well-being?

Where in my life should I put myself first but do not?

What kinds of things can I do to honor my priorities going forward?

Creative Prescription Tools and Activities

This section covers *Creative Prescriptions* tools, journal questions, and activities to help you explore things that are preventing you from making yourself a priority. Select the topic(s) you need in this moment to create your own prescription.

When You Don't Feel Worthy

> *When you tap into your creative well spring, you make your happiness a priority and take your worth seriously.*
> —Rebecca Schweiger, *Release Your Creativity*

I think the biggest obstacle to not making ourselves a priority is feeling that we are not worthy of taking this time for ourselves. We let everyone else's priorities come before ours. Self-worth is an important part of your foundation for healing and well-being. If you don't feel you are worthy of self-care, you will not do what it takes to regain your health. Many women in our society think their self-worth is connected to their productivity or physical beauty. It is hard to maintain your self-worth when it is based on exterior things.

The good news is that you can replace feelings of unworthiness with creativity! In a study in the *Journal of Health Psychology* (2006), researchers Collie, Bottorff, and Long, stated that art-making "brings a sense of personal worth." When you create, you defer to an inner reference source; you are guided by your soul. And your soul is not dependent on the opinion of others! Your soul knows your worth, and it cannot be measured in this materialistic world.

> *When you're soul-centered, you are not dependent on others for your sense of self worthiness.*
> —Sarah McLean, *Soul Centered*

If there is ever a time to be soul-centered, this is it! In the mist of all your struggles with illness, you are worthy of love and are worthy of being taken care of. You are also worth the time you take just for yourself, for when you create, it pays you back with joy, contentment, and stress relief. This is necessary when going through cancer treatment. The following is a client story on how not feeling worthy affected her ability to make the best health choices.

Client Story

I had a health-coaching client who was a woman in her late fifties with diabetes and high blood pressure. We worked together on improving her health by setting goals to make healthier food choices and exercise. During the workweek, she did well with her lifestyle changes, but on the weekends, she always struggled because there were family events and celebrations that involved a lot of fried foods and greasy cheese casseroles that she could not stop herself from eating.

One week she told me that she was going to her daughter's wedding. I suggested we talk about a game plan to help her eat healthy food during the wedding because there would probably be many things to eat that she could not resist. The client stated, "I am not going to have a problem eating healthy this weekend because during the wedding, I'm going to take care of my granddaughter, who is four. That child is precious to me, and we're going to eat off the same plate, so I am not going to let anything unhealthy touch her lips."

I looked at the client and gently stated, "It's wonderful that you love your granddaughter and only want to feed her the healthiest foods. Is it possible for you to see yourself and your own body as precious too? Is there any way you can treat yourself in the same loving manner, by only giving yourself the best, whether or not you are with your grandchild?"

The client thought for a few moments, her eyes welling with tears, but she could not say it; she could not say that she could treat herself in the same loving way. She could not say that she was worthy of being treated as someone who was *precious* too.

This is so sad, yet I find that this is true with many of my clients. Feeling worthy is about honoring yourself and treating yourself like the *precious person* that you are! The following activity will help you tap into this feeling.

Activity: Precious Self

Make a copy of a photo of yourself when you were a little girl. If you do not have one, use a current picture. Paste the image in the center of the following page. Around the picture, write your answer to this question: **How do you want to care for this precious little girl?**

How do you want to care for this precious little girl?

Journal about the experience by answering the following questions:

How did I feel after doing this activity?

Growing up, what were the rules or beliefs in my home about being worthy or deserving? Do I still believe this?

Going forward, what decisions can I make from a place of "How can I love and cherish myself more?"

When You Need to Say No

You can be a good person with a kind heart and still say no.
—Lori Deschene

Making yourself a priority sometimes means saying no to people in our lives. Why is it so hard for women to say no? Many of us were taught that we were "selfish" little girls when we said no to the requests of others! I know I was told this as a little girl, and I was made to feel ashamed of myself. Many women are afraid that family members will become angry if they say no to them, so they agree to things in order to "keep the peace." Others feel they don't have a right to voice their feelings or opinions. *Is it any wonder why women are afraid to say no?*

Was there ever a time when you said yes to something you *truly* did not want to do in order to be polite and later regretted it? These types of yesses drain your energy, and you need to use your energy to recover your health. Every person has personal boundaries, and when we are not allowed to voice them, we feel invalidated and disempowered.

I know that sometimes it is hard to say no, but if you can allow yourself to feel uncomfortable for a few seconds, it will spare you from feeling used or resentful in the future. Remember that every time you say no to something that you do not want to do; you are making space for saying yes to something that does serve you. You have every right to say no, so don't feel guilty about expressing this right. Be polite but firm, and remember you are not responsible for the other person's reactions.

As women, we need to have boundaries or everyone else's needs will take over our time. Cancer strips away everything that is superficial and unimportant, so focus on your own needs. This is a good time to think about your priorities and your boundaries because they have probably changed since your diagnosis. Use your cancer diagnosis as your permission slip to say *no*. I love the way Sarah Ban Breathnach talks about boundaries in her book *Simple Abundance*. She states, "We want our lives to feel limitless, so we must learn the art of creating boundaries that protect, nurture, and sustain all that we cherish." Now, does that sound selfish or self-centered to you? Is it selfish to "protect, nurture, and sustain what you cherish" ... which is *you*!

Activity: Learning to Say No

Stand in front of a mirror and practice saying no to common things that people ask you to do:

Practice saying, "No, I'm sorry, but I will not be able to help you with that." or "No, I have plans that day." Keep it simple. This will help you avoid feeling guilty or having to justify your answer.

Sometimes we need to say no to people in our lives that drain us or don't support our healing. For people you don't want to see, say, "I am sorry I can't see you right now. I'm focusing on my treatment and recovery."

Journal Questions:

How do I feel about saying no to a request?

What activities or people have I said yes to in the past that I am now going to say no to?

What chores or responsibilities can I hand over to another person so I can focus on my own needs and healing?

When You Need Permission to Choose Differently

> *I had a wonderful time during my recovery, there was this fabulous excuse to do all the things that were good for me, all the things that cause me joy and happiness. I had cancer. I could change whatever I'd liked, do whatever I needed, I had a great reason, a great excuse.*
> —Ian Gawler, *You Can Conquer Cancer*

I love the above quote from Ian Gawler because he used cancer as a reason to justify making his happiness a priority in his life. There are few upsides to having cancer; however, one of them is being able to make different choices for yourself. This is one of the few times in your life that you may feel that you have the *right* to do whatever you need to take care of yourself. You have a right to reset your priorities, to change your life to suit your needs, to say no to everything you do not want in your life, so do it!

You have, as Ian Gawler puts it, a "fabulous excuse to do all the things" that are good for you and bring you joy and happiness. He had a wonderful time during his recovery from stage IV cancer! Can you imagine that? *I truly want you to imagine that.* People will expect you to be different after a cancer diagnosis, so take this opportunity to make the changes you have been wanting to make.

Activity: Expressing My Power of Choice—Free Pass

You have a free pass to change your life for the better if you so choose, so use it!

Free Pass

Going forward, I am giving myself permission to do all the things I have been wanting to do.

I have a free pass to _____

And _____

And _____

And _____

And _____

And _____

When You're Lacking Self Love

When I loved myself enough, I began leaving whatever wasn't healthy. This meant people, jobs, my own beliefs, and habits – anything that kept me small. Now I see it as self-loving.
—Kim McMillen, *When I Loved Myself Enough*

If you don't love yourself, you will not make your needs a priority! Having cancer makes you realize how precious life is. All the things you did not love about yourself, like your *thunder thighs*, fall away during cancer treatment. Self-love comes from accepting yourself exactly as you are right now, sick and scared, perfectly imperfect. True self-love comes from being at peace with who you are, with all your faults, personality traits, and yes, even your cellulite.

When you love yourself, you can be authentic, which is an emotionally healthier and empowering way to live. The more you love yourself, the better you will take care of your body. Learning to see and talk to yourself in a loving way is a crucial step to wellness. The following client experience is a beautiful story that illustrates a tender way to show yourself and your body some love during cancer treatment.

Client Story

A coaching client who, after much thought, decided to go forward with chemotherapy treatment. She had been feeling fearful before she made her decision, but once she made the decision to proceed, she was confident that it was the right choice. The night before she started her first chemotherapy treatment, she decided to have a little talk with her body. She said the following things to her body

"Listen, I know that you are afraid about starting chemotherapy tomorrow, and I want you to know I am here for you. I really believe in this doctor and in this treatment plan, so I know this is the best option for us. I promise to take good care of you while undergoing chemotherapy. I want you to know I love you and I will make sure that you have plenty of time to rest and ensure that you are well fed. If there is something that you need, just let me know, so do not be afraid; I am here for you. We can do this together!

Activity: Love Letter to My Body

Write a letter of love and encouragement to your body that you can read before you enter any treatment.

Journal Questions:

How is my self-love reflected in how I take care of myself right now?

What thoughts of self-appreciation would help me love myself more in this moment?

What little things can I do or say to affirm the love I have for myself every day?

Activity: What Do I love about Myself?

Learning to love yourself and your body is essential for healing and wellness. This love will help you make lifestyle changes that are more nourishing and health promoting. One of the rewards of creativity is that it promotes *self-love* because you accept, respect, and honor your unique expression in this world. In the following exercise, write down the things you love about yourself. Do not be modest; go for it! Be like Macrina Wiederkehr, a Benedictine nun who said, "O God, help me to believe the truth about myself, no matter how beautiful it is!"

Enjoy coloring the following picture to remind yourself that you are loved by others too!

When You Lack Self-Compassion

> *Compassion isn't a self-improvement project or ideal that we're trying to live up to. Having compassion starts and ends with having compassion for all those unwanted parts of ourselves, all those imperfections that we don't even want to look at.*
>
> —Pema Chodron

I have included the section on self-compassion because I saw that many clients were very compassionate with others but did not extend the same compassion to themselves.

What Is Self-Compassion?

Merriam-Webster's online dictionary describes compassion as "sympathetic consciousness of others' distress together with a desire to alleviate it." Based on this definition, *self-compassion* is a sympathetic consciousness of your own distress and the desire to alleviate it.

Self-compassion is not about feeling sorry for yourself. It is about acknowledging your own suffering without fear because you also have the tools to self-comfort and self-care. Self-compassion allows you to identify where you are suffering and take active steps to alleviate it. Being compassionate with yourself is just as important as any vitamin, diet, or exercise program for your health.

Self-compassion allows you to be an empathetic observer of what you are thinking and feeling, without triggering the stress response. For example, if you are waiting for the results of a lab test and you are starting to become anxious, you can say, "I am starting to feel anxious, so I'm going outside to walk and get some fresh air." While you are walking, you can acknowledge that you are suffering and you can be open to thoughts of nurturing self-care and wisdom. It is easier to face difficult health issues when you know you have the tools of self-compassion to comfort yourself.

> *The essential element in nurturing our creativity lies in nurturing ourselves.*
>
> —Julia Cameron, *The Artist's Way*

Creativity can enhance self-compassion too. In 2017, the Intentional Creativity Foundation conducted a survey within their community and other artists' circles and found: "92% of the people surveyed felt that creativity influenced [increased] their compassion for themselves."

Mandalas as a Healing Tool

> *Creating mandalas offers a visual manifestation of a positive intention that can inspire and empower us in our daily lives. Each mandala that we create is as unique as the person who creates it.*
> —Kathryn Costa

Mandala coloring books are popular for a good reason: they provide centering and calming benefits. *Mandala* is a Sanskrit word that means "circle" or "center." It is an ancient symbol for wholeness. Making a mandala is basically creating an image within a circle that is an expression of what is within your soul or your self-knowledge.

> *Working within a mandala that represents your universe gives you a healthy starting point for your self-exploration.*
> —Vicky Barber, *Explore Yourself through Art*

We can use mandalas to connect to our intuitive wisdom in a safe and contained space. Creating a mandala can lead to better health and well-being because it is a doorway to understanding what you need, allowing you to practice self-compassion.

Activity: Self-Compassion Mandala

In her book *Self-Compassion*, author and researcher Kristin Neff uses a beautiful mantra when she is in pain:

> This is a moment of suffering.
>
> Suffering is a part of life.
>
> May I be kind to myself in this moment.
>
> May I give myself the compassion I need.

Color in the following mandala and quote. When done, answer the following journal question.

This is a moment of suffering.
Suffering is a part of life.
May I be kind to myself in this moment.
May I give myself the compassion I need.

Journal Question:

How can I show myself more compassion while I am in treatment?

When You Are Tired of Being Strong

Sometimes making yourself a priority means saying, "I am tired of being strong for everyone else." Many women suppress their feelings to stay strong for their families. They put on a brave face to make everyone else comfortable. This takes a big toll on their emotional resources and health. *Being strong is not about denying what you are experiencing!* It is about turning toward the unpleasant feelings, acknowledging you are suffering, and doing something about it. This is how you build resilience.

Research on resilience shows that people who are more compassionate toward themselves have a lower incidence of depression and anxiety over the course of their lifetime. Not acknowledging our suffering can cause us to become worn down and exhausted over time, which makes it even harder to "stay strong." Know that it is perfectly fine to say you don't feel strong, if that is what you are experiencing. Let your family know so they can step up and support you in your needs.

In addition to the activity that follows, go to the previous section under "When You Need to Be More Compassionate with Yourself" for more tools.

Activity: Transforming Suffering into Strength

You can transform/transcend your suffering into strength by acknowledging you are suffering and take action to alleviate it. One way to acknowledge and alleviate pain and suffering is using creative expression. In India, yogis (practitioners of yoga) create art for transcending suffering. Take a little bit of time for yourself and color the following picture. While coloring acknowledge the ways that you are suffering, and listen to the promptings of your body, mind, and soul, on how you can alleviate the pain. Fill in the following drawing and complete the sentences:

Right now, I acknowledge that _____.
In acknowledging this, I can alleviate some of the pain by _____

Right now I acknowledge that_____

_____

In acknowledging this, I can alleviate some of the pain by

_____

Journal Questions:

How did I feel while doing this activity?

What insights did I gain?

What can I do to increase my self-compassion?

When You Want to Explore Your Creative Medicine

> *The act of creating empowers us to have a say on how we will shape and respond to the suffering and hope within us.*
>
> —Catherine Moon

When I was an emotionally pain-ridden teenager, creating art and journaling was my only relief from emotional pain. My art was my *medicine*, and I made it a priority in my life. Creativity provided me with a safety net that supported me during difficult times. My art-making, gave me the nourishment that I needed at that time, that I was not receiving from my home environment.

Dr. Bernie Siegel, author of The *Art of Healing,* believes we receive the most healing benefits from the creative process when we are in the "zone." Being in the zone is when you are focused on an activity and time falls away; you feel energized and fulfilled in body, mind, and spirit. You do not need any training or talent to get into the zone, you just have to allow yourself to be *present* while focusing your attention on one thing. Your *creative medicine* can be, raw art journaling, doodling, gardening, or coloring with your kids. Everyone has their favorite thing that makes them go "aah."

When you make creativity a priority while you are in treatment, you give yourself access to the healing benefits of creative expression. I saw firsthand that coaching clients who incorporated creativity while in treatment developed better coping skills. They used creativity as a tool to manage stress, depression, and worry. When you *create* with the *intention* to explore the healing benefits, you use creativity/art-making as a type of *medicine.* For the purposes of this book "healing" is defined as *restoring your own personal sense of balance and well-being.* The following story shows how one client had a better quality of life because she used her art-making as her creative medicine.

Client Story

A coaching client found the Creative Prescriptions activities so helpful that she decided to start her own art group with her friends. Creating art in a group setting reduced her isolation, helped her forget about her treatment, and contributed to her feelings of well-being. I saw many of the pieces that she created. They were powerful images about her life and her cancer journey. Even though she was in treatment, she made creativity a priority because of the many healing benefits she would not have experienced otherwise.

Enjoy coloring the following drawing

Activity: Creative Medicine Drawing

What is my creative medicine?

What activities feel restorative? What activities energize me? What feels healing? What do I love to do? What activities relax me? What brings me joy?

Journal Questions:

What benefits do I experience while being creative?

How can I use creativity to support my healing process?

Does my hospital offer art therapy classes? What classes can I attend online?

What is my creative medicine?

When You Need to Take Better Care of Yourself

Self-care is not selfish or self-indulgent. We cannot nurture others from a dry well. We need to take care of our own needs first, so that we can give from our surplus, our abundance. When we nurture others from a place of fullness, we feel renewed instead of taken advantage of.
—Jennifer Louden, *The Woman's Comfort Book*

Self-care, as defined by en.oxforddictionaries.com, means the following: "The practice of taking an active role in protecting one's own well-being and happiness, in particular during periods of stress." This definition is interesting in that it uses the word *protecting* when defining self-care. I agree that as women we need to protect our self-care time because it is necessary to our own "well-being and happiness." I do believe self-care should be part of your treatment plan. Dr. William B. Stewart, author of *Deep Medicine*, states it simply and beautifully in the following quote: "Self-care is primary care."

Self-care is making your needs a priority in your life. It's having an attitude of "my needs matter too," and it is an essential part of your healing process. Self-care is about refilling your well so you are not functioning from a depleted state.

To be healthy, you must make a conscious decision to say *yes* to yourself and schedule self-care time into your daily or weekly activities. Put yourself first on the list, not last or at the end of a long day. How you take care of yourself is one of the few things you can control in your life. It is your job to take good care of yourself so you can model that for your loved ones. Do you really want to teach your daughters to put themselves last? You can spend self-care time with someone you love too. Before we go forward, let's explore your beliefs about self-care.

Journal Questions:

What was I taught about spending time on self-care as a little girl or teenager?

How does my upbringing affect my views on self-care today?

As an adult, how can I reframe my thoughts about "self-care" so it feels right for me?

Self-Care Retreat

> *Self-care is not self-indulgent, self-care is self-respect.*
>
> —Jody Day

We all need to have mini-retreats on a regular basis! All of us are running around stressed out, drained, depleted, and undernourished, and then you add cancer into the mix. Planning a mini-retreat will help you reset your priorities. It will make you realize how important it is to stop, be still, and go inward to nourish and replenish your beautiful self.

My Story

When I was writing this section, I came down with the flu. I was so sick and drained and had absolutely no energy, and then I realized that this was perfect. I'd do a mini-retreat for myself!

My mini-retreat included starting the day with prayer and meditation. Normally I would go for a walk in the morning, but I did not have the energy to do that, so I just walked into my backyard and sat there for ten minutes enjoying the sunshine and the flowers in the garden. Then I made myself a cup of tea with honey and drank it while I soaked in a tub of Epsom salts and lavender essential oil for my aching body.

I also gave myself a clay mask facial because I love the scent of the earthy clay; my skin likes it too. This made me feel pampered. For lunch, I did not have the energy to cook, so I made myself a green smoothie and then sat outside and colored a mandala.

Even though I did not feel well physically, emotionally I was happy that day because I felt very nourished, loved, and well cared for.

This is an example how even if you are not feeling well you can do little things that promote feelings of well-being. In the following activity, you will ask yourself, *What does my body, mind, and spirit need right now?* and plan your retreat around that answer. Or you can set an intention for the retreat: "My intention is to feel peaceful, renewed, inspired, nourished, or happy." Then plan the activities around your intention.

Activity: Planning My Retreat:

Take a moment to close your eyes and take a few deep breaths. Go inward and ask yourself, *What kind of retreat does my body, mind, and spirit need right now?* or *What is the intention of my retreat?* Write down what comes to mind and design a retreat around those ideas. I have included a beautiful drawing with the affirmation **"Self-care is self-love"** for you to enjoy coloring on your retreat.

My Mini-Retreat

For my body

Things that make me happy!

'For my spirit...

Self-care is Self-love

CHAPTER 5

Creative Prescription 3: Express Yourself

When you're holding on to anger, you have less room for love.
When you're holding onto resentment, you have less room for happiness.
When you're holding on to fear, you have less room for creativity.
—Nick Ortner

Emotions versus Feelings

Being diagnosed with cancer can be an emotionally overwhelming experience, causing fear and anxiety, due to the anticipation of the pain from treatment and an uncertain future. This is a normal reaction for someone diagnosed with cancer, so it's important to be honest with yourself about your feelings. I found that many of my clients denied or suppressed their feelings because they did not want to upset their family, but consider this: if you do not feel it is safe to share your feelings with your family, they will not feel it's safe to share their feelings with you either. This can add more stress to an already difficult situation. *When we deny or suppress our feelings, we cannot give ourselves the compassion and kindness that we need to take care of ourselves.* If your family is not good at communicating, consider going into family counseling so everyone can learn how to express their feelings in appropriate ways.

For the purposes of this book we will be using the findings of neuroscience research for the definitions of emotions and feelings:

Emotions are biochemical and electrical reactions in the body that create a physical response. Emotions are hardwired into every individual and are responses to internal or external stimuli.

Feelings arise from emotions. The frontal cortex gives meaning to the emotions based on our personal experiences, beliefs, and learned responses.

In other words, emotions are *physical* sensations, while feelings are our *interpretation*s of the emotion.

Neuroscientist, researcher, and the author of *Molecules of Emotion: The Science behind Mind-Body Medicine,* Candace Pert, PhD, states, "The chemicals that are running our body and our brain are the same chemicals that are involved in emotion. Thoughts and emotions bubble up from the body to the brain, where we can process and verbalize them according to our expectations, beliefs, and other filters." This means that we experience emotions in the *body* as well as in the head, but the brain assigns the meaning in the form of thoughts and feelings. However, sometimes things are not so clearly defined, *fear* is a good example of this.

Emotional expression of fear is a physical reaction to a specific source of danger. Our hearts automatically begin to race, and our muscles contract. This happens unconsciously. However, fear can be triggered by remembering a scary event, and it can have the same physical reaction as the initial experience.

Feelings can be expressed as fear: "I am afraid of the side effects of treatment," or it can be associated with anxiety such as the fear of flying or the fear of speaking in public.

An emotion like fear can be a learned behavior. For example, if your mother is afraid of dogs, you may learn to be afraid of dogs from her behavior.

Emotions and feelings are not always easy to categorize. However, emotions are usually fleeting. We may feel emotional pain when we find out we have been deceived, but it will subside. However, the *feelings and thoughts* surrounding the betrayal may continue to cause emotional pain. This is what creates suffering! Suffering is optional

> *Forces beyond your control can take away everything you possess except one thing, your freedom to choose how you will respond to the situation.*
> —Viktor Frankl, author and Holocaust survivor

Emotions and Health

> *Creativity is the perfect balm to sooth a lot of what ails you.*
> —Rebecca Schweiger, *Release Your Creativity*

We are complicated emotional beings. This is not something we can change, nor should we want to. Emotions have an important job. Our emotions help us to understand ourselves and what is important to us. I love what Karla Mc Lean states in *The Language of Emotions:* "Our emotions, especially the hidden and squelched and despised ones, are our direct link to inner wisdom." They are an aspect of our body's intelligence sending us information.

Denying or suppressing your emotions can lead to "dis-ease," such as short-term digestive issues, headaches, and fatigue. Long-term suppressed emotions can lead to chronic illness. In a study published in the *Journal of Psychosomatic Research* (2013), research done at the University of Rochester and by psychologists from Harvard School of Public Health indicated that "suppressing emotions may increase the risk of dying from heart disease and certain forms of cancer."

Neuroscientist and researcher Dr. Candice Pert said, "My research has shown me that when emotions are expressed … all systems are united and made whole. When emotions are repressed, denied, not allowed to be whatever they may be, our network pathways get blocked, stopping the flow of the vital feel-good unifying chemicals that run both our biology and our behavior." Dr. Pert believes that in order to have good health, *all the emotions* need to be expressed in *appropriate* ways.

When experiencing health issues, it helps to learn how to channel difficult emotions in a manner that supports us, and our relationships. This is where creative expression can come in, as one way to express emotions in a safe, appropriate, and contained manner.

Note: Always seek the help of a professional therapist if emotions become too hard for you to handle by yourself.

The Benefits of Using Creativity to Explore Emotions

> *Art helps us to look at our shadows so they can be understood and healed.*
>
> —Doreen Virtue, *The Courage to be Creative*

Art-making is an amazing process for channeling emotions in a safe and appropriate way. To use it as a self-care tool, use your emotions to enter the creative process and ride the wave of that emotion. Creative expression gives you a new language with which to express your emotional world. For example, when I was a frustrated and angry teenager, I could take my emotions out on a chunk of clay allowing me to channel and transform that energy, into a piece of pottery. While you are going through a difficult time, consider making time for regular art breaks as part of your treatment and wellness plan.

You can use art to help you relax around your diagnosis of cancer because art can help you manage the emotional difficulties of treatment. Expressing your emotions in this creative manner can help you to reduce stress, self-soothe, and create positive feelings, thus restoring balance to the body, mind, and spirit. Art-making gives you a say on how you want to express your emotions, which is cathartic and empowering. You do not have to understand or interpret your art to have a healing experience.

A study done by the *Journal of Psychology of Aesthetics, Creativity, and the Arts* found the following: "Art-making was an effective way of venting feelings about problems." In another study, published in the *Journal of Health Psychology* (2006), by researchers Collie, Bottorff, and Long, found that the art-making process allowed participants to "see" what they were feeling. It stated, "It led to other things, such as acceptance, resolution, empowerment, healing, decision, and reduced fear."

Expressing Your Emotions

> *When nothing is planned, you only have your own feelings with which*
> *to begin. Is it nothing or is that everything?*
> —Michelle Cassou and Stewart Cubley,
> *Life, Paint and Passion*

It is important to not suppress or deny your feelings during cancer treatment because this can suppress the immune system and reduce the energy you need for healing. Let the art-making process be a space where it feels safe to openly express (or vent) your feelings. It takes courage to sit with unwanted or unpleasant feelings, but if you can do this, and channel those feelings through your creativity, you can reduce emotional pain.

The first step of tapping into the healing benefits of creativity around your emotions and feelings is that you must acknowledge them. By expressing and accepting the strong emotions/feelings you have, they lose the power to affect your life in negative ways. Creative material allows us to express these feelings from a place of curiosity so the emotions and feelings no longer feel scary or overwhelming. Art-making allows us to use our emotions and feelings as creative fuel! If you are angry, frustrated, scared, lonely, or happy, use all these feelings as the raw fuel for your creativity. So, let's explore our emotions with honesty, openness and curiosity in the activities that follow.

Note: Always seek the help of a professional therapist if emotions become too hard for you to handle by yourself.

Creative Prescriptions Tools and Activities

This section covers *Creative Prescriptions* tools, journal questions, and activities to help you explore and address emotional issues in a creative container (this book). Select the topic(s) you need in this moment to create your own prescription.

When You Are Angry

> *Let us not look back in anger or forward in fear, but around in awareness.*
> —James Thurber

You have to feel your emotions in order to heal them. When my clients are diagnosed with cancer many of them feel angry, and frustrated, and need a tool for dealing with these strong emotions. A study published in the *Journal of Health Psychology* (2006), by researchers Collie, Bottorff, and Long, about art therapy and art-making, found that for some of the participants "Physical movement was the key [for] releasing or getting rid of feelings."

I agree that doing something "physical" is a quick way to move these emotions/ feelings through you and out of your body. Of course, the physical activity cannot be harmful to yourself or others, so I encourage you to do it with your "art." The study mentioned a participant named Laura, who described herself as "someone who does not let her aggression out" yet found it "satisfying" to be "physical, rough, and destructive with her art."

The following exercise is a quick anger/emotional-release activity you can do anywhere. As stated previously, when you allow yourself to feel emotional pain, realize that the pain is not permanent. The emotions are fleeting when we experience them fully. Research shows that *physiologically, emotions last around ninety seconds*. That's it! Emotions will dissipate in ninety seconds if you don't create a story about the pain. In this activity, you will be scribbling out your anger or frustration for at least ninety seconds or until you feel better.

For strong emotions, use several blank sheets of paper. Feel free to scribble, to rip, to crumple up and throw the paper. Do what feels "satisfying" to you.

Activity: Releasing Anger

Use a pencil or marker and scribble out all your feelings on this page. Aah, doesn't that feel better? Repeat if necessary.

Aah, that felt good! Your turn

Annette Tello, M.S.

When You Are Feeling Anxious

The *Journal of the American Art Therapy Association* did a study (2005) titled "Can Coloring Mandalas Reduce Anxiety? The study examined different types of art activities to determine if they could reduce anxiety. The participants were randomly assigned into three groups.

Group 1: unstructured- randomly drew on a blank piece of paper.

Group 2: colored a plaid design,

Group 3: colored a mandala.

The results indicated that "Anxiety levels declined approximately the same for the mandala-and plaid-coloring groups and that both groups experienced more reduction in anxiety than did the unstructured-coloring group. These findings suggest that structured coloring of a reasonably-complex geometric pattern may induce a meditative state that benefits individuals suffering from anxiety." Color the following image the next time you feel anxious. There are more tools for anxiety and other emotions in the activities that follow.

Activity: Coloring for Anxiety Relief

Take some time to enjoy the relaxing and meditative benefits of coloring, by coloring the image that follows.

When You Need an Emotional Self-Care Plan

Art explains our feelings to us.
—Samantha Bennett, artist

You can use art-making as a tool that focuses on a theme for emotional release—for example, releasing frustrations, fear of going through chemotherapy, and so on. This is an activity I developed for my workshops to help participants manage difficult emotions. In part 1 of this activity, you will identify an emotion or feeling and the corresponding behaviors. In part 2, you will create a plan of action for the emotion/feeling, allowing you to respond with self-compassion and kindness.

Activity Part 1: Identifying Emotions, Feelings, and Behaviors

Supplies: colored pencils or felt markers

Select one emotion or feeling you would like to work on.

Use the following blank page to write down the feeling you want to explore. For example, if you want to explore your feelings of anxiety, write the word anxiety in the middle of the page in large letters.

Then recall a time when you felt anxious and write down, what you felt and what you did, around the word anxiety. Be conscious of your automatic responses and patterns of behaving. For example: anxiety: I feel nervous, jittery. I get impatient, quick to anger, feel frustrated, make poor decisions (and so forth). Do this now then go to the journal questions and step two.

Journal Questions:

What normally triggers this emotion or feeling?

If my emotion/feeling could talk to me, what would it say?

In what ways can I take better care of myself next time I feel this emotion, and show myself some compassion?

Activity Part 2: My Emotional Self-Care Plan

In this part of the exercise, you will develop your personal self-care plan of action.

For example, the next time I am feeling impatient or jittery, I know these are symptoms of my anxiety and I can do the following:

- Choose to turn toward the feelings—holding them in awareness until they subside
- Take my notepad out and scribble until the jitters are gone

- Do a breathing technique to calm my nerves, showing my self-compassion and kindness (we will learn breathing techniques in chapter 7)
- I can remove myself from the situation that caused it

In this plan, I am showing myself compassion and ways to take care of myself.

My Emotional Self-Care Plan

This technique can be done with each emotional pattern that you would like to address. Next time you feel this emotion, what will be your plan of action?

Next time I feel _____, I will:

1.

2.

3.

4.

You can have a self-care plan for all your emotions/feelings:

If I am feeling sad, I will ...

If I am feeling frustrated, I will ...

If I am feeling lonely, I will ...

If I am feeling angry, I will ...

If I am feeling _____, I will ...

If I am feeling loved or happy, I will savor it!

When You Feel Lonely

People crave comfort, people crave connection, people crave community.
—Marianne Williamson

When we are sick, it can be soul crushing to suffer all alone. When we understand that pain is part of the human experience and we realize that whatever we are going through, many others have gone down this path before us, we do not feel so alone. If you can recognize that your feelings are part of the human experience, you will be more open in sharing your feelings with others. In a group of shared experiences, we can see ourselves in others, allowing us to feel compassion for them and extending that compassion to ourselves. A strong sense of community can evolve very quickly, in part through the witnessing of each other's journey.

> *What is most personal is universal.*
> —Carl Rogers

Research shows that being lonely and isolated is not good for your health. My experience has been that clients who are isolated and alone have a higher chance of becoming depressed. In Dr. James Gordon's book *Unstuck,* he states, "When you let yourself feel the sadness or rage that gets stuck and buried in depression and you share those feelings, you are no longer depressed—pushed down and flattened out. You are expressing yourself and connecting with someone else." He believes that *expressing* yourself will help you to move forward if you are stuck in depression. He uses tools like journaling, drawing, breathing exercises, and nutrition to help patients with depression.

In the activity that follows, think of people you know who can be part of your support system, your tribe, that can help to reduce your feelings of loneliness.

Activity: My Tribe

In addition to having people help with meals and drive me to appointments, who in my tribe can I call to:

Keep me company

Uplift my spirits

Pray with me and for me

Make me laugh

Watch my favorite movies with me

Support Groups

I encourage all of my coaching clients to join a cancer support group. Even if they have loving and supportive families, they may still feel as though they don't have anyone that understands what they are going through. When I ask my clients, what has brought them the most comfort during their treatment, the majority say being with other women who are going through the same thing.

In a support group, you are allowed to share your fears and anxieties in a safe and supportive environment. Having social support is sometimes the only thing that keeps us going through difficult times. A support group also gives you the opportunity to be a support to others. Most hospitals offer cancer support groups, so don't suffer in silence. Check them out. If you cannot travel, there are many online support groups on Facebook, and some cancer organizations can connect you to a peer who has recovered from the same type of cancer.

Resources for over-the-phone support:

Cancercare.org—Offers free counseling and support groups by oncology social workers who provide emotional support to anyone diagnosed with cancer.

Imerman Angels (imeramanangels.org)—Provides free one-on-one cancer support for cancer fighters, survivors, and caregivers.

Memorialcare.org—Offers a Women-Guiding-Women program, a peer-mentoring program for newly diagnosed breast and gynecological cancer patients.

Activity: My Social Support

Make a list of groups you can join for companionship, support, and social activities— for example, clubs, meet-up groups, church prayer groups and so on.

1.

2.

3.

4.

Creative Community

Consider joining a creative community to combat loneliness. As women, we are always looking for connection, and meaningful relationships and art-making groups or classes can offer us an avenue to these. Creating in a group setting is a great option to reduce isolation and have uplifting social interactions, plus it helps you to be more creative.

Client Story

A coaching client who lives alone makes every effort to attend the weekly art class offered at her hospital, no matter how she is feeling. She states that it gives her a chance to get out of the house and socialize with other cancer patients in a relaxed and supportive environment. She also stated that the class stimulates her creativity, and afterward she would go home and continue creating, providing her with hours of enjoyment and relief.

I attended an art therapy class held at a local hospital with one of my coaching clients. I had expected the class to be emotionally heavy and sad; however, I was pleasantly surprised to see all the cancer patients happily talking to one another as they worked on their creative activities. There was a lot of camaraderie, laughter, and joy in that class. At the end of the class, the patients had an opportunity to share their work. While I listened to everyone's stories, I learned that this classroom was a "haven" for them. This was a place where they could forget about their cancer and pain by getting into their creative zone, a place where they could attend to their own emotional needs and self-soothe.

The participants had made artwork that was meaningful to them, and I was reminded that making art was about *making meaning* in our lives. When illness disrupts our lives, the need for "meaning-making" increases, giving us a sense of our unique value and purpose. This is so important when many patients lose their individuality in the medical system. I could see why the patients told me they looked forward to coming to this class.

Many hospitals and cancer centers are now offering art therapy classes. They offer emotional and creative support in the company of other cancer thrivers. Making art in a group setting allows you to be seen and heard while facilitating social connection. *But remember that studies show you don't need to be in art therapy to receive the therapeutic benefits of art-making!* If your local hospital does not have art therapy, ask a friend to host an arts and crafts night for you. You can hang out with other creative people without focusing on yourself and your illness. Being able to share something you all enjoy in common can create a sense of community and enhance well-being.

Activity: Creative Prescriptions Group

To belong to a tribe of like-minded individuals, join our *Creative Prescriptions* group, which is an online art community on our Facebook page, Fb.me/creativeprescriptions.

When You Are Fearful

> *I've been absolutely terrified every moment of my life—and I've never let it keep me from doing a single thing I wanted to do.*
> —Georgia O'Keeffe

Fear is probably the predominant emotion for cancer patients; the fear of pain and an uncertain future can keep you up all night. Going into treatment can be scary! I had a client refuse all conventional treatment because of the fear of the side effects and pain. When out-of-control fear keeps you from following through on your treatment, you must address your fears for your health and survival.

Experiencing fear is going to be a part of your cancer experience, but it does not need to dominate your journey. Not all fear is bad; it can protect you and keep you safe. *Realize that we are genetically wired to have fear as a survival mechanism.* It is good to have respect for our fear; however, we are not meant to live our lives in fear, letting it make all our decisions.

> *I've learned as time passes, all the things that you're afraid of will come and they will go, and you'll be alright.*
>
> —Stevie Nicks

If you suppress your fears it can drain your energy and your vitality. This is precious energy that you can use to heal your body. If you face your fears, they will have no power over you. When you confront and understand your fears, you will realize that they are not as terrifying as you originally thought.

Our fears will always be with us because fear is part of our survival instinct, so it is important to learn how to manage our fears rather than letting them manage us. In the following activity we are going to form a new relationship with our fears. As stated in the introduction in Dr. Michael Samuel's book *Creative Healing,* he describes how art heals: "Our physiology changes from one of stress to one of relaxation, from one of fear to one of creativity and inspiration."

Note: If you have had traumatic experiences, consider working with a therapist.

Activity: Being the Boss of My Fears

This activity is about being the boss over the fears that are keeping you from living to your fullest and healthiest potential. It is about using creativity to communicate with your fears in a new way. You can do this by playing with art supplies that will allow you to bypass your left brain and tap into the wisdom of your right brain and your body.

Being comfortable with how your body feels while experiencing fear-based thoughts and feelings will allow you to take the reins of the emotion before it overtakes you. We all have heard of the expression "Feel the fear and do it anyway." I am going to add that you feel the fear, you acknowledge it, by saying something like, "I know you're here and we are going to be okay," then do it anyway. Many of my workshop participants have had powerful and transformational experiences with this process. I hope that you do too!

Note that you do not need to know how to draw to do this activity. This exercise can be used with any emotion or feeling you want to explore.

Supplies: colored pencils or pastels, plus a piece of paper the size of a business card

Part 1

Take a moment to close your eyes and take a few deep breaths. Feel your feet on the floor and the ground beneath them. Be present and feel your inner body. Take whatever amount of time you need to feel present and grounded.

Then think of the situation that is causing you to feel fearful. What physical sensations are you having about the fear? Notice **where** you are feeling the fear in your body. Focus your attention on that area of your body, then ask your body for an image of your fear.

What is coming up? What does your fear look like? What images come to mind? Does it have a color, shape, or texture to it? What does it "feel" like?

Stop when you feel ready and take a moment to draw or scribble the **essence** of what you experienced. When done, look at the image and answer the following journal questions using **your nondominant hand** so you can access the information from the body.

Journal Questions:

Ask your fear, "Why are you here? What is your purpose?"

If my fear (or any emotion/feeling) could speak, it would say …

My message(response) to my fear is …

Part 2

Once you have completed the above activity and have answered the journal questions, take the small piece of paper and draw a symbol or a sentence that reflects your new understanding of your fear. This will help you acknowledge it, but that you are the "boss." You can use one of these phrases to help you gain control: "You're not the boss of me." "You can come on this journey to recovery with me, but you can't drive." "I see you and acknowledge you, but I make the decisions."

Pull out the small piece of paper the next time the fear pops up. Keeping your fears out in the open for you to "see" causes them to lose their power.

This activity allows us to take something that is internal and move it to the external, where we can see it in a new light, where it is not so scary.

When You Need to Lean into Emotional Strengths

Strength doesn't come from what you can do. It comes from overcoming things you once thought you couldn't.

—Rikki Roger

A friend going through treatment told me, "When you are feeling brave, it is easier to face treatment like chemotherapy." This is true. Treatment can trigger our fears and anxieties, but once we acknowledge them, we can use the tools in this chapter, to tap into our strengths.

This activity is to remind you that you have inner strengths that you have used in the past to overcome other hardships. You were brave in the past, and you can tap into that memory to give you strength today. Once you have completed this activity, remember these strengths by reading them to fortify yourself during your treatment and afterward.

Activity: Remembering Past Strengths

Know this: You already have the skills to cope with your current stressors.

Take a moment to recall a past crisis or hardship and journal briefly about what happened and how you resolved it/conquered it. Then answer the journal questions that follow.

Journal Questions:

What did I learn from the situation?

What inner strengths did I use to overcome the situation?

What strengths do I have that I can lean on during treatment?

Activity: Powerful Drawing

In the image that follows, Place a picture of yourself in the center of the drawing to remind yourself how powerful you are, then color in the drawing. If you like, cut it out and place it somewhere you can see it every day.

When You Want to Be the Heroine of Your Own Life

The clients I have had the honor to serve have been strong and amazing women! However, many of my clients undervalue the strengths that they have used to overcome many difficulties in their lives. Qualities like kindness, responsibility, compassion, generosity, and so on, are strengths too! You can be your own superheroine by acknowledging your strengths to remind you of how **awesome you are!** You can be the superheroine of your own life.

Activity: I Am My Own Heroine

Around the image of the superheroine, write down all of your "superpowers" and then color in the image.

Write down your "superpowers" around the image then color it in.

When You Want to Feel Happy!

Today I continue to art journal because it puts me in touch with my own joy.

—Samantha Russo, artist

The research in the field of positive psychology has identified three pathways to happiness: pleasure, engagement, and meaning. Creative endeavors can contain all three. Making art can bring people the *pleasure* of playing with different mediums. That is why the paint and party classes are so popular; they are a lot of fun. I have seen the participants in my classes express joy and happiness in playful creative exploration. Making art *engages* you in the enjoyment of the moment. Even if you do not create a "beautiful" work of art, what you create can have a purpose and be *meaningful* to you.

In the book *The Happiness Advantage,* author and researcher Shawn Achor lists positive habits that anyone can implement to increase their personal happiness. He recommends "gratitude, journaling, exercise, and meditation" as habits we can build to increase our happiness. Of course, I would add "creative self-expression" to that list. ☺ All these habits are discussed in this book in the following sections:

· **Gratitude:** When You Need to Cultivate a Positive Mind-Set
· **Journaling:** When You Need a Tool for Processing Your Cancer Journey
· **Exercise:** When You Are Feeling Fatigued
· **Meditation:** When You "Should" Be Meditating but You're Not

My Story

When I was in my last semester of my senior year of undergraduate school, the psychology students were required to participate in a happiness study given by one of the professors. At the end of the semester, the professor had the results of the study, and he gave out three certificates of recognition for the happiest students in the study. To my utter surprise, he called out my name as one of the happiest students in the study!

Wait, what? Me? I never considered myself a happy-go-lucky person! Up until that time, I had been a very introverted and serious person, and I was shocked that I was happier than all the outgoing, sociable, smiley-faced students that surrounded me in class. But then, as I thought back over that semester, I realized that because I had completed my requirements for my psychology degree, I had two extra electives (classes), so I took a ceramics class and a photography class. Every day that semester, I had a class that allowed me to spend time being creative.

Looking back, I see that the art classes allowed me to release the stress of school and spend time on activities that brought me a lot of joy—and apparently made me one of the happiest students in the psychology department! This helped me recognize that there was a direct correlation between my happiness and making art, and I have research results that prove it!

For me, creating not only makes me happy; it fills me with inspiration, vitality, and energy. Creating takes me out of my head and negative thought patterns, allowing a sense of wonder to return to my life. I also savor the feelings of happiness when I feel it.

Research shows that whatever a person's situation, rich or poor, educated or not, it has minimal effects on their ability to be happy, for happiness is an inside job. Being happy or cultivating happiness is a choice, and creativity is one way that we can choose to cultivate happiness. Getting lost, or in the zone, during a hands-on activity increases happiness and improves ones psychological well-being. Barry Jacobs, PhD, of Princeton University, found that repetitive movements, such as those used in creative projects, enhanced the release of serotonin, relieving symptoms of depression.

Studies show that creativity does increase happiness and improve mental health. The *Journal of Positive Psychology* (2018) had a study article titled "Everyday Creative Activity as a Path to Flourishing," and it states, "Recent experience sampling and diary studies have shown that spending time on creative goals during a day is associated with higher activated positive affect (PA) on that day. Overall, these findings support the emerging emphasis on everyday creativity as a means of cultivating positive psychological functioning." In other words, creativity makes us happy!

Activity: My Happiness Project

List creative activities that help you cultivate your happiness/positive psychological functioning:

1.

2.

3.

4.

5.

Make it your goal to find ways of incorporating these things into your life on a regular basis.

When You Need Things to Look Forward To

Going through cancer treatment can be an arduous journey. For clients, that journey can be made easier by having something to look forward to, like a son's graduation or the birth of a grandchild. Research shows that having something to look forward to, increases the pleasure of that thing. *In delaying instant gratification, we promote pleasurable anticipation.*

In the following activity, we are going to make a list of the things you are looking forward to after you have completed treatment. It can be a big thing like going on vacation or little things you have been wanting to do, such as taking cooking classes. Savor the pleasure of looking forward to doing it.

Activity: I Am Looking Forward to ...

Color the following image and then list the things you look forward to doing when you are done with treatment.

Things I look forward to:

CHAPTER 6

Creative Prescription 4: Manage Your Mind-Set

The mind has the power to make an inert medicine work or a good medicine seem inert.

—David Hamilton, PhD

Healing Starts in Your Mind

You are not always going to feel positive while in treatment, however, you can consciously choose to cultivate a positive mind-set that will help you during recovery. Learning to use your mind to your benefit will become the powerful resource it was meant to be.

A research article published by the *National Science Foundation* in 2005 stated that of the thoughts we have during the day, "Eighty percent are negative thoughts and ninety-five percent are repetitive thoughts." This study shows how much time and energy we spend on useless thoughts!

Studies have shown that what we think about our treatment has an impact on our recovery; therefore, we should be *aware* of our thoughts. Cancer specialist Dr. Francisco Contreras believes "there is a direct connection between the mind and cancer because immune suppression is a direct result of emotional thought." Promoting a positive mind-set will support your immune system, uplift your moods, and increase overall feelings of well-being.

So how do we shift our mind-sets? In the book *The Upside of Stress*, the author, Kelly McGonigal, PhD, shows through research that the most effective mind-set interventions have three parts:

1. Learning a new point of view
2. Doing an exercise that encourages you to adapt and apply the new mind-set

3. Having an opportunity to share the new idea with others

In the activities in this chapter, you will learn new ways of shifting your mind-set, and you will experience it in the exercises that are included in each section. You will have the opportunity to share your experiences in a supportive community on the *Creative Prescriptions* Facebook page at fb.me/creativeprescriptions.

Creativity to Shift Your Mind-Set

Creative expression is a great way to shift your mind-set. Our brains are wired for creativity! The PBS show *The Evolutionary Advantages of Art,* shows how humans are hard-wired to make *art,* check it out on pbs.com. You can use creativity to support you as you experience the ranges of thoughts and emotions that are a part of the treatment and recovery process. Studies have shown that creativity is an effective tool for decreasing depression and anxiety for cancer patients.

In the art-making process, what you are thinking and feeling is made visual. This process allows you to consciously observe parts of you that were hidden, making room for reflection, growth, and transformation. Art-making gives you the space to explore emotional thoughts, allowing you to rewire your brain's neural pathways, thus reducing negative thought patterns. The following story is a good example of how creativity can help you change a negative mind-set.

Client Story

One of my coaching clients shared with me that when things did not go well in her treatment or in her life, she frequently became very negative. Her inner "mean girl" came out and would keep her in a negative self-talk mode for hours at a time, if she let it. She would tell herself things like, *You're so stupid. Why didn't you …* She found the easiest and fastest way to shift out of her negative self-talk was to pick up her art supplies and just start playing with the materials. This distracted her from her self-deprecating commentary and provided a most effective way to stop her negative mind-set; in addition, she had amazing art journals!

This story is a great example of instead of fighting your negative mind-set, use your creativity to silence it. I love artist Trish O'Malley's quote: "When you are creating you are not a victim." Creativity helps us avoid being a victim of our negative thought patterns. *The mind always needs something to think about,* creativity helps us to focus the mind on the task at hand—your creative project. When negative thoughts pop up when you are creating, focus your mind on the materials you are using, how they feel in your hands, and the physicality of the experience. This will develop your self-awareness of the present moment and interrupt negative thoughts. To change our negative thought patterns, we must first identify or label these patterns. The following activity will help you do that.

Creative Prescriptions Tools and Activities

This section covers *Creative Prescriptions* tools, journal questions, and activities to help you explore your thoughts and cultivate a positive mind-set. Select the topic(s) you need in this moment to create your own prescription.

When You Have "Stinkin' Thinkin'"

Don't make your cancer recovery more stressful on your body by adding negative thinking or "stinkin' thinkin'" to the process. Before you can change your thoughts, you need to be aware of your thought patterns. Sometimes you can think yourself into anger, depression, and anxiety without even realizing it. Once you can identify your negative thought patterns, you can step back from them and see them as they really are, just thoughts that have no power over you.

Just because we think something, does not mean it is *true*. "Name it to tame it" is a phrase coined by author and psychiatrist Dr. Daniel Siegel. As soon as you can name the thought pattern, you have stopped yourself from being caught up in the drama. This will let the brain's frontal cortex take over. The frontal cortex, the center of higher reasoning, helps you make the decision on whether the thought is true and if you should act on it. I tend to overreact to situations, so I call my overreactive thoughts my "drama queen." This *naming*, or label, stops me from acting out from an overly emotional state. Once you are familiar with your emotional patterns, it will be easier to stop letting negative thoughts and emotions ruin your day.

To help you from being caught up in the drama of your own thoughts, take some time to recognize your most common thought patterns. Note: the colors associated with each pattern will be used in the next activity.

Awfulizing (yellow):	We exaggerate and blow things out of proportion.
Controlling (blue):	We want things a certain way—our way.
Condemning (red):	We become the victim and blame everyone for our problems.
Worrying (green):	We worry about future events that may never happen.
Ruminating (purple):	We ruminate about the past, over things we cannot change.
Obsessive thoughts (orange):	We think about the same thing repeatedly.
Low frustration level (gray):	Everything gets on our nerves.

Activity: What Is My Stinkin' Thinkin'?

Supplies: Colored pencils, in the colors listed above

This exercise is an easy way to become aware of what type of thinking you most predominantly use. Write down your most prevalent negative thoughts on the balloons, then color over them with the corresponding stinkin' thinkin' color. For example, if your thought is a "worry" thought, color that balloon green. When you have completed this activity, answer the questions that follow.

Write down your most prevalent negative thoughts on the balloons, then color over them with the corresponding stinkin' thinkin' color. Add more balloons if you need them.

Journal Questions:

What is my most predominant "stinkin thinkin"?

How are these thoughts affecting my recovery?

Now that I know my predominant negative thoughts, how can I reframe those thoughts next time I have them?

I will practice my reframing and share my new insights with …

Annette Tello, M.S.

When You Want to Be More Mindful in Your Life

Mindfulness is a tool for managing your mind-set. Being *mindful of your thoughts* will help you reduce the worries and uncertainty you have about your life and illness. If you can *stay present and not focus on the future,* you will do much better during your healing process because mental thoughts that stress you, drain your energy.

Mindfulness helps us to accept what we are thinking and feeling and use self-compassion to get us through difficult situations. During times of stress, mindfulness gives you space to consciously choose how you want to think and behave in the moment. To be mindful, we need to set the daily intention of focusing on the *present* with awareness.

On dictionary.com, mindfulness is defined as:

1. The quality or state of being conscious or aware of something
2. A mental state achieved by focusing one's awareness on the present moment, while calmly acknowledging and accepting one's feelings, thoughts, and bodily sensations, used as a therapeutic technique

When we are worried about our problems, it helps to come *back to our senses.* Research from Professor Mark Williams at Oxford University shows that an effective way to ease out of unhelpful thinking is to pay attention to our *direct sensory experience.* This means paying attention to our felt senses, like tightness in the body, shallow breathing, and so on. This simple tool brings us back to our body and the present moment, calming the mind. Here is a beautiful example of that:

Client Story

"While I was standing in the kitchen doing dishes, I was worrying about my pending chemotherapy treatment. I suddenly noticed I was holding my breath and my stomach muscles were tight while I was feeling a wave of anxiety. I realized that I had felt like this before but never paid attention to it nor even was aware I was doing this. I held on to the kitchen counter and took deep breaths for a few minutes. This helped relax my stomach muscles and it relieved the feeling of anxiety. From that moment on, I made sure to be more mindful of my body and muscle tension to manage my worries and anxiety."

This client became mindful that she was worrying and that it was causing her to hold a lot of muscle tension. Once she became *aware* of this, she acted by taking a few deep breaths to relax her body, taking care of what she needed *in that moment.*

When you are mindful, you are in touch with your inner wisdom, which helps you to make decisions that are nourishing to your body, mind, and spirit.

Ways of practicing mindfulness can include being *aware* while you do daily activities such as taking a shower or washing dishes. When you take a shower, enjoy the warm water on your skin and the scent of the soap to make you mindful of that moment. Cultivating awareness, or mindfulness, teaches us to slow down and appreciate and enjoy the little things in life. This is not hard to do—just do what you are doing with more attentiveness and focus.

Research shows that creative engagement offers the same benefits of mindfulness, reducing stress and the anxiety caused by worry. When we worry, it is because we are afraid things will not turn out the way we want them to. *Art-making is an access point to the present moment.* Art-making helps us experience the mindfulness practice of nonattachment, which means letting go of the thought that things need to be a certain way. We learn to make "mistakes," let go of our expectations, and go with the flow.

> *My art journaling has helped me through many difficult times in my life, mostly with the day to day things [and] it helps me be more present and observe things around me that, before, I never saw.*
> —Tiffany Goff Smith, journal artist

The following activities will help you reduce your worry about the future and learn how to focus on the present moment. Photography can help you look at the world through a different lens. It can help you to stop and look at the world around you, paying attention and accepting the life that is right in front of you.

Activity: Mindfulness Selfie

Activity: Mindfulness Selfie

Take a selfie and answer the following questions:

In this present moment I am_____

_____

In this moment I see_____

I hear_____

I feel _____

I accept_____

Activity: Personal Mantra

Mantras are sacred words or phrases. A *personal mantra* is a phrase or affirmation you can use for inspiration or for focusing your mind on something positive, such as "all is well," or "I can do this." Mantras have been shown to calm worrying thoughts and anxiety.

Add your personal mantra to the center of the following image. While you are coloring, repeat the mantra. The next time you are worried, repeat the phrase in a soothing rhythm until you feel calm and at ease again.

Journal Questions:

What activities in my life can I use to experience mindfulness?

How does it feel to be mindful?

Would a mindful practice be beneficial to me while undergoing treatment?

When You Need to Calm the "Monkey Mind"

The mind is very powerful, so why don't you use that power for healing? Most of us have what Buddhists call a "monkey mind." A monkey mind scatters your thoughts and energy all over the place activating the fight-or flight-response. Having a mind that is clear and calm will lead to the release of healing hormones that support the immune system, enhancing your body's ability to repair itself.

When I was in yoga training, I learned that it was difficult to maintain a balancing pose if my thoughts were scattered. I learned that in order to maintain my balance,

I had to *focus* on a fixed point and my breath, which allowed me to calm my mind and maintain my physical balance.

> *Breath awareness is a tool that has transformational powers. You can literally change your mind and your mood just through the breath.*
> —Baron Baptiste, *Perfectly Imperfect*

To calm the monkey mind, it helps to keep your *gaze steady and focus on your breath*. Focusing on your breath can shift your attention away from obsessive and unpleasant thoughts by bringing your consciousness to the present moment. When we are stressed, our breathing becomes shallow or rapid, which can lead to increased feelings of anxiety. The breath is one of the easiest ways to bring our body, mind, and spirit into sync.

The following activity is a great tool for people who feel they are unable to calm their thoughts, their monkey minds. Focusing on one thing will help you connect inwardly and calm your mind. This is something you can do anywhere, even in a doctor's office waiting room.

Activity: Drawing the Breath

Supplies: Pen or colored pencil

Sit comfortably in a chair and notice your feet touching the ground and pressing against the floor. Place your pen down on the following blank page and have a soft gaze as you look at the paper. Then notice your breath, without any need to change it. As you breathe, start moving your pen to the rhythm of the inhalation and exhalation. See if your body and breath can work as one.

If your thoughts wander to something other than your breath, **stop and make a little dot with your pen.** When your thoughts come back to the breath, you can move your pen again. Stop and make a dot every time your thoughts wander off the breath.

Do not worry about how many dots you have on the page; the purpose of this activity is to train your mind to be conscious of when it wanders off (scattering your energy) from what you are doing.

Journal Questions:

Was this activity able to calm my mind? If not, why not?

Was I able to feel *present* as I was moving my pen to the breath?

Could I reduce the number of dots with regular practice?

When You Need a Tool for Processing Your Cancer Journey

I think journaling is one of the most important tools for processing our thoughts and feelings during treatment, and that is why I made it a part of the *Creative Prescriptions* process. Journaling lets you put your illness in perspective, helping you to realize that cancer is not who you are. Journaling also allows you to come to terms with your cancer in your own way and at your own pace. Journaling (writing and visual) is an important part of the *Creative Prescriptions* process. It is how we:

- Express and acknowledge our thoughts and emotions
- Process and integrate our experiences

- Connect to our intuition and wisdom
- Gain new insights and clarity

Journaling allows you to "see" negative thought patterns that affect your mind-set. This is valuable because you cannot change things that you do not allow into your awareness. When you become aware of these patterns, you realize that awareness is the greatest agent for change, and it opens the door to personal growth and transformation.

> *Keeping a journal stimulates awareness and mental clarity; offers you the opportunity for creativity; provides comfort; and promotes emotional healing.*
>
> —James S. Gordon, MD, *Unstuck*

What Is Journaling?

Journaling is your personal account of events, your thoughts, and the emotions of your daily life. Journaling can include visual expression with images and other art mediums.

Cancer Support Group Story

I saw firsthand the power of journaling for healing. As I was getting ready to present a journaling workshop to a cancer support group, a few members returned from the hospital and informed us that one of the group members was not doing well. Understandably, everyone in the group became upset. I took that opportunity to talk about how to use journaling as a tool for expressing emotions.

I gave all the women lined notebooks and asked them some open-ended questions to answer. One question was how they felt about their friend, and what fears it brought up in them. I also asked them to think about what they could do to self-soothe or take care of themselves. Afterward, the women had a chance to share what they had written.

There were many tears and a lot of love and healing that took place in that group because they were able to share their feelings and fears in a community of women who were experiencing the same thing. I completed the workshop by giving the women art supplies and stickers to decorate and personalize their journals. The women left feeling happier; the journaling allowed them to unburden themselves by expressing their feelings, while thinking about self-care, and the fun of decorating their journals lifted their spirits.

The Research on the Benefits of Journaling shows that it is especially helpful for people who may have a hard time talking about their thoughts and feelings with others. A study done at the University of California found that participants who wrote down their feelings were better able to "regulate their emotions."

The *Journal of Advanced Nursing* (February 2013) published the conclusions on a journaling study and stated, "Expressive writing, focusing the instructions on writing about one's living and dealing with a diagnosis of breast cancer, is recommended for early breast cancer survivors as a feasible and easily implemented treatment approach to improve quality of life."

Naming and writing about your emotions helps to put the brakes on the fight-or-flight response. In the *Journal of Psychology & Health* (volume 17, 2002), a study on expressive writing states the following: "These findings indicate that expressive writing has a wide range of social, emotional, and physical health benefits for individuals coping with stressful events, particularly if they are experiencing ongoing intrusive thoughts and avoidance responses related to the stressor."

The therapeutic benefits of journaling come from making it a regular practice, so it helps to establish a routine. When you journal on a regular basis, it allows you to explore and experience new ways of thinking about your situation. The act of writing occupies the left side of the brain, allowing the right side of the brain to express itself more freely. This allows you to tap into your stream of consciousness, where you can access your own voice, your own wisdom, thus helping you to experience new ways of knowing yourself. You can use journaling as a form of self-care and observation of health-enhancing patterns.

> *My art journaling time is in fact self-care and restorative.*
> —Nancy Lefko, artist

If you are *resistant* to answering the questions after the activities, then write about that—about why you are resisting. You can also override the resistance of the logical mind by writing with your nondominant hand while answering the questions. Try this at least once to experience it. There is no right or wrong way to journal.

Activity: Personal Journal

Purchase a personal journal that you can use on a daily basis to gain the therapeutic benefits mentioned above. Use the journal for the following coping tool.

Activity: Daily Brain Drain

Cancer will give you many emotional ups and downs, and the daily brain drain is an effective way to dump all your emotions out of your body and onto the page. This tool allows you to release negative thoughts and emotions and unburden yourself. When you write your truth, you can open yourself up to new perspectives and insights.

Don't worry about spelling or grammar; it's about releasing emotional tension. You can be creative and use images, colored pens, and markers if you like.

Every evening, take ten to fifteen minutes to write down everything that occurred today that bothered you. For your first brain drain activity, have fun dumping your thoughts onto the following image!

Other Option:

If you do not know what to write about in your journal, consider using

sentence stems, a sentence-completion process. Complete the following sentences:

Right now, I feel _____.

Right now, I think _____.

I really want to _____.

Note: Always seek the help of a professional therapist if emotions become too hard for you to handle by yourself.

Annette Tello, M.S.

"Brain Drain"

When You Need to Cultivate a Positive Mind-Set

Gratitude unlocks the fullness of life. It turns what we have into enough, and more. It turns denial into acceptance, chaos to order, confusion to clarity.

—Melody Beattie, author

Gratitude is one of the best ways to cultivate a positive mind-set! I think that gratitude is the antidote to many of life's sorrows. When we are ill, we can focus all our time on treatment and recovery, forgetting to enjoy and be grateful for the little things in life that touch our hearts. When we do not feel well, it is hard to be grateful because having cancer or any chronic illness can leave us feeling so stressed and vulnerable. Researcher and author Brené Brown states, "If you want more joy in your life, you have to practice gratitude, especially in those moments of vulnerability."

A case study focusing on gratitude with breast cancer survivors found that women who had higher levels of self-reported gratitude experienced less depression, stress, and irritability. The key is in focusing on what is good in your life and appreciating it. I believe that when you are in a state of gratitude, it opens you up to love and miracles. Life is comprised of small moments of time that make up what really matters in life, like random acts of kindness, laughing with others, and appreciating the beauty that is all around us. These things give us moments of sweetness that we can savor, if we take the time to notice them. When you see the good in life, then what you see expands.

Dr. Jon Demartine feels that "gratitude releases *unconditional love*," which promotes physical, mental, and emotional healing. In his book *Count Your Blessings*, he shares these wonderful affirmations that you can use to cultivate a positive mind-set:

I am grateful, my heart is open, and the healing power of unconditional love is filling my body.

Both my health and my sickness are blessings and opportunities for me to love myself and others.

Other affirmations:

I am grateful for my body and all that it does for me.

I am grateful for the healing abilities of my body.

Gratitude Journal

A gratitude journal is an affirmation of everything that is good in your life. It helps you identify things that nourish and support you and that you want to increase in your life. When I was having a hard day at work, I would look at my gratitude wall. This was a wall by my desk where I had pinned all my thank-you cards, letters, and emails from my clients. It reminded me of why I was there, and it never failed to lift my spirits.

I know it may be difficult to keep a gratitude journal when you are feeling so crappy. However, if you give it a chance, it may help you spend less time thinking about negative stuff. The creative act of writing in a gratitude journal also reduces stress and increases your sense of emotional well-being.

The secret to the gratitude journal is to be grateful for something different every day. Looking for the good things happening around you will decrease the amount of time you spend complaining and being unhappy. I used to be a very negative person, until I started a gratitude journal. Now I look for things to be grateful for. This keeps me focused on appreciating the good in my life.

How to keep a gratitude journal: Use your personal journal and every night think of three things that you are grateful for that day. It may be something someone did that was kind; maybe it is being grateful for a beautiful day. Whatever it is, this practice will help you develop a gratitude for all the things great and small in your life.

Another option is to begin every day writing about the three things from the day before; this will start your morning on a positive note, which you can take with you throughout your day. The more time you spend thinking of the good things in your life, the happier you will be. You can also add cards, quotes that inspire you, and emails with words of love and support, to your journal.

Activity: My Gratitude Journal

For a week, write down your moments of gratitude. The following questions will help you get started on your first week:

Who made me laugh today?

Who did a random act of kindness for me this week?

Who gave me a loving hug?

Who made me a home -cooked meal this week?

Who took me to treatment this week?

Who gave me a beautiful smile today?

Who called or texted me to tell me how much they love me?

Date _____
Today I am grateful for,
_____
_____
_____
_____
_____
_____

Date _____
Today I am grateful for,
_____
_____
_____
_____
_____
_____

Date _____
Today I am grateful for,
_____
_____
_____
_____
_____
_____

Date _____
Today I am grateful for,
_____
_____
_____
_____
_____
_____

Journal Questions:

When I focus on gratitude, do I notice a change in my mood or mind-set?

Do I think it would be helpful to continue a daily gratitude journal?

Activity: Gratitude Collage

Supplies: Photos, glue stick, scissors, markers.

Create a gratitude collage on the following blank page, by adding some photos of things you are grateful for and why.

Annette Tello, M.S.

When You Have Chemo Brain

Many of my clients worried because they were becoming forgetful during treatment. They would forget where they parked the car or left their keys. To help them, I suggested practicing mindfulness. You will not remember where you put your keys if your mind was not paying attention to the keys to begin with. The majority showed great improvement in their memories when they practiced mindfulness (see "When You Want to Be More Mindful in Your Life"). Try practicing mindfulness for your chemo brain; it does help.

Research done in a senior living facility in Great Britain showed that patients who engaged in artistic expression during middle age through old age were seventy-three percent less likely to have problems with their memories or cognitive impairment. *Outcome data showed that drawing activated the brain centers that sharpen memory and created new neural connections.* Great! We can use creativity to combat chemo brain.

Activity: Creating New Neural Connections

Let's draw something easy, like doodles, to create new neuron connections in our brains!

When You Want to Remind Yourself How Loved You Are

The following activity came from a coaching client, and it touched my heart, so I had to share it with everyone!

Client Story

A client who was going through chemotherapy shared with me that she has a scrapbook in her home that she uses as an art journal. When her family comes to visit from out of town, they each take turns at creating a page. The family members paint, draw, collage, and write words of love and inspiration for the client. The love that is in this journal gives her comfort. It reminds her how loved she is when her family is not around.

Activity: Love Scrapbook

Buy a scrapbook or art journal at your local craft store. Have art supplies available so that when friends and family come to visit, they can create a page for you. Look at your scrapbook whenever you need a boost to your spirits and a reminder of how precious and loved you are!

CHAPTER 7

Creative Prescription 5: Connect to Your Body's Wisdom

I tried to give myself something to think about other than how awful I felt so I started painting again. In the process of creating, thoughts about pain, loss and sorrow diminished.

—Lisa Brown, author

Benefits of Creativity on the Body

Your body is a miracle that allows you to have a physical experience on this earth. When you break a bone, the doctor will set the bone and give you a cast, but he is not doing the healing—your body is. Cancer will shake your trust in your body; therefore, learning to love and trust your body again is part of the healing process. While in treatment, it is important to know what supports your body's healing and incorporate that into your life.

Research shows that creative activities that use your hands, help to decrease stress and relieve anxiety. Barry Jacobs, PhD, of Princeton University found that *repetitive movements, such as those used in creative projects, enhance the release of serotonin, relieving symptoms of depression.* Serotonin also improves moods, increases feelings of happiness, and reduces anxiety.

There are hundreds of studies documenting the physical benefits of the creative process on the body. These studies show that the creative process reduces stress, lowers blood pressure, improves immune function, and it can even reduce pain! A study done at the Mayo Clinic and published in the *European Journal of Cancer Care* showed that patients that participated in a creative process had "significant improvements in positive mood and [reduced] pain scores ..."

As stated in the introduction, Shaun McNiff, art therapist and the author of *Art Can Heal Your Life,* writes about how creating is all about *energy.* He describes the circulation of creative energy as a part of the art-making process that provides healing to the body. If your body is tight and constricted, your creativity and your ability to tap into this energy will be constricted too. Allow yourself to be open and free in your creativity in order to tap into the "energy" that is available to you, without expectations that it will be a certain way.

> *By paying attention to our physical self through collage and journaling, we allow the body to have a voice.*
> —Lucia Capacchione's book *Visioning: Ten Steps to Designing the Life of Your Dreams*

Creative expression is a way to give "voice" to your body. The creative process is an avenue for tapping into your body's inner knowing; it offers a line of communication between the body and the mind. Creativity helps us to be open to exploring new avenues for healing. In this chapter, you will learn creative ways of connecting to your body and accessing its voice to promote healing and well-being.

Creative Prescriptions Tools and Activities

This section covers *Creative Prescriptions* tools, journal questions, and activities to help you explore your body's wisdom and ways to heal through the creative process. Select the topic(s) you need in this moment to create your own prescription.

When You Are Stressed Out

> *Even if stress isn't an obvious contributor to the onset of a disease, stress management often becomes a relevant aspect of recovery in a comprehensive treatment plan.*
> —William B. Stewart, MD, *Deep Medicine*

What is stress? Stress is the emotional and physical way in which we respond to pressure. Stress can be environmental, physical, emotional, or psychological. The brain and the body do not distinguish between a *real* or an *imagined* threat. Therefore, thinking negative thoughts that create an emotional reaction will trigger the "stress" response in the body.

Getting cancer is stressful! Of course, this is a normal and understandable reaction. It affects every aspect of your life; it changes your life whether you want it to or not. The stress of cancer will activate the fight-or-flight response, which causes hormones such as adrenaline and cortisol to be released into our bloodstream, causing a spike in blood pressure and an increase in heart rate, which we don't need when we are trying to heal.

The good news about stress is that new studies are showing that there are positive benefits to having stress in your life! In her book *The Upside of Stress*, Kelly McGonigal, PhD, wants us to change our concept of stress. She states, "Stress is what arises when something you care about is at stake." If we did not care about anything, we would not have any stress, but would we really want to live this way?

Research done by Alia J. Crum of Yale University showed that embracing stress and seeing it as a positive motivator for what is important to you can increase your DHEA. DHEA is a neural steroid that physically protects you from the damaging effects of the stress hormones and enhances immune function. Therefore, it's important to cultivate a positive mind-set about stress, which in turn helps the body respond with an increase of DHEA. How you think about the stress can determine whether you thrive under the stress of cancer or become anxious and fatigued. Her studies showed that people who did not believe stress was bad for them had less depression, more energy, and fewer health problems.

In another study done by Crum, with the employees of a Fortune 500 company, she found that to be successful in changing your mind-set about stress, it helps to do the following:

1. Acknowledge that you are experiencing stress and how it effects your body.
2. Allow the stress because you are responding to something you care about.
3. Think about how you can use the energy that stress is giving you.

In the activities that follow, we are going to explore how stress affects our bodies, how we feel about stress, and how to use that energy to focus on what we want— or how we can channel the energy in a more positive way. We may not be able to control all the stressful events of our lives, but we can control how we think about stress and therefore affect how our bodies respond to it.

Recognizing, accepting, and managing stress is an important part of recovery and can be part of your treatment plan. The first step in managing stress is learning to listen to your body. Tuning into how your body is feeling will let you know the first signs of stress. When you recognize the early signs of stress, you can stop negative thoughts and reframe your situation, then use the energy for self-compassion and self- care.

Activity: Stressed-Out Body

This activity will help you understand how stress affects your body.

Tune into your body while thinking about your stressful situation and in the following outline of a body, color in the areas where your body is holding the stress. Make a list of your symptoms, such as muscle tension, and headaches, and where in the body you are feeling it. Once you complete the activity, answer the journal questions that follow.

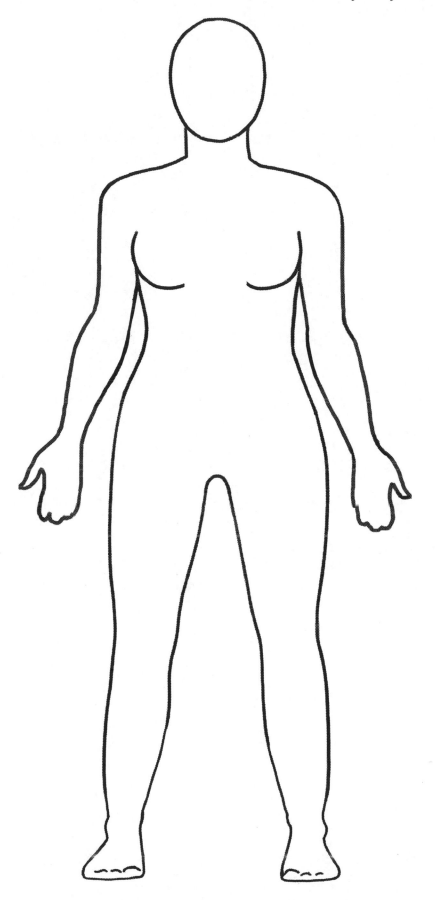

Journal Questions:

After completing the previous activity, where is my body holding stress?

What are my current perceptions about stress and its effects on my health?

How can I see my stress as something positive, that it is a response to things that I really care about?

How can I use the energy behind my stress to motivate me to make health-enhancing changes in my life?

One way to channel your stress energy is to engage in creative activities. Making art has been shown to reduce stress by facilitating relaxation. In a study published in the *European Journal of Cancer Care*, Dr. Jack Lindh states, "Women who participated in an art therapy group that had been diagnosed with major stresses due to breast cancer showed significant improvements in the reduction of stress..."

Activity: *Creative Stress Busters*

Make a list of three creative activities you can do to channel your stress energy:

1.

2.

3.

When Cancer Takes Your Breath Away

Cancer can take your breath away, but breathing techniques can anchor you back into your body. Focusing on your breath grounds you, helping you to feel centered, and safe in the present moment. When we engage in conscious breathing techniques, we can activate the "relaxation response." In his book *The Wellness Book*, cardiologist and researcher Herbert Benson, MD, describes the relaxation response as a physiological state characterized by a "slower heart rate, rate of breathing, lower blood pressure, and slower brain wave patterns." The relaxation response, also called the "rest-and-renew" response, releases healing hormones like oxytocin.

I did not know how important the breath was to my health until I was in training for my yoga teacher certification. Most of us are unaware of our breathing, but the breath is a good indicator of our stress level. Every emotion has a corresponding breath pattern. When you are anxious, observe your breath. How is it different from when you are sad? Or happy? When you are feeling anxious and ungrounded, ask yourself, *How am I breathing?* This will direct your attention away from your thoughts, to your body and the present moment.

Breathing patterns reflect our emotional state, and *conscious breathing* activities can change those states. You can consciously reduce your breath rate to activate the relaxation response. Breath rate/frequency is the number of times we do a complete breath—inhale and exhale—per minute. Most people have a breath rate of about twenty breaths per minute. Lowering your breath rate to eight breaths per minute will bring you to a meditative state. Deep breathing lowers your breath rate and sends a signal to the brain that you are calm and safe, activating the rest-and-renew state of the body. The following activity will help you reduce your breath rate to activate the relaxation response.

Activity: Drawing My Breath Rate

Set your watch or phone timer for one-minute

While breathing normally, draw a star for every breath you take on this page. At the end of one minute, count the stars. This is your breath rate per minute.

Set the timer for another sixty seconds and continue to draw a star for every breath. This time see if you can slow your breathing rate. See if you can reduce the number of stars each time you do this activity.

Activity: Tracing the Breath

This activity helps to reduce stress by mindfully tracing the petals of the flower, in the following image, as you consciously breathe. As you retrace the petals, move your finger slower and slower to deepen the breath.

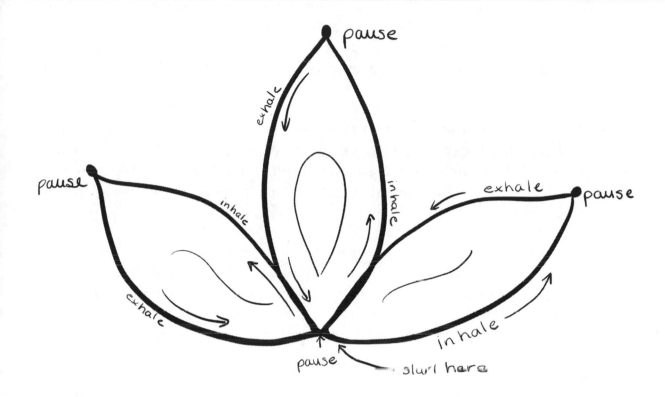

When You Feel Disconnected from Your Body

> *For fast acting relief, try slowing down.*
> —Lily Tomlin

I truly believe the increase in health problems in our country is due to the disconnection to our bodies. There are television commercials saying, "Don't let heartburn or an upset stomach stop you from eating whatever you want." Really? If you have an upset stomach, your body is trying to tell you something! This type of thinking leads to a disconnection from your inner wisdom (your body), which can lead to illness.

What if, instead of taking an antacid tablet and going on with your day, you stop to think about what is causing your upset stomach? Am I eating foods that are not good for my body? Or maybe the tension I am feeling is affecting my ability to digest my food? Am I feeling unsafe in this moment? Or maybe I ate too fast because I am always in a rush?

Medication suppresses symptoms so we can go on with our day with minimal disruptions. If you take it on a regular basis, you never take the time to explore the reason you are not feeling well, and the body will continue to get sicker and sicker until it is heard. That is why it is important to have a daily practice of tuning into your body if you want to heal and stay healthy over the long term.

Try the body scan exercise in this section several times in different situations to help you form a deep connection to your body and its needs. As you become more in tune to what is going on inside your body, you will be able to recognize symptoms of "dis-ease" before they develop into a more serious health issue. The body changes from day to day, so if possible, make it a daily practice.

Before you do the body scan, let's explore how you feel about your body in the following exercise and journal questions.

Activity: How Do I Feel about My Body?

Use a pencil and answer the question "How do I feel about my body?" Write your answers inside the body image. Then answer the journal questions about the changes in your body since diagnosis.

How do I feel about my body?

Journal Questions:

After completing the activity, what did I learn about myself and my body?

How have my feelings about my body changed since my diagnosis?

Can I accept and love my different body?

The Wisdom of the Body

Neuroscientist, researcher, and the author of *Molecules of Emotion: The Science Behind Mind-Body Medicine,* Dr. Candace Pert said something interesting in an interview. She said that based on her research, she believed that the "subconscious mind was the body communicating with the brain." She felt the whole body contained the wisdom of what we considered to be our "subconscious mind." If that is true, then we should be connecting to our bodies to understand the subconscious messages that are waiting to be heard.

A body scan is a way to experience *somatic awareness* which means learning to feel your body, to help you identify physiological and psychological factors for promoting healing. The body scan is a tool to help you tap into the subconscious needs of your body. Body scans will also help you make better health and life style choices.

Client Story

A coaching client loved the body scan tool that I shared with her. She did this scan every morning to determine how she would plan her day. Every day she had activities that included the self-care of her body, mind, and spirit. For example, to take care of her body on a "good day," she went for a ten- to twenty-minute walk. On a "bad day," when she could not get out of bed, she did some gentle stretches in bed.

I love that she started the morning tuning into her body and had different options depending on how she was feeling that day. She was able to use this tool to make progress while honoring where she was physically and emotionally *on that day*. When you know how you are feeling first thing in the morning, you can plan activities based on the needs or capabilities of your body on that day.

Activity: Daily Body Scan

This guided body scan will help you to connect to the wisdom and messages from your body. The guided body scans can also be used to ground and center yourself.

Take a deep breath through your nose to the count of four.

Hold your breath to the count of four (without tightening the body).

Exhale through your mouth to the count of six.

Do this four times.

Then continue breathing regularly as you start the scan at the top of your head and go down the body. Be present as you focus on the sensations of your inner body.

Start by scanning your head.

Then go down to your neck and shoulders,

Moving down to each arm and hands.

Then focus on your chest, then move down to your abdomen.

Continue moving down to your hips, then down each leg, to your feet and toes. Feel the floor beneath your feet to keep you grounded in the present moment.

As you scan your body, tune into any areas where you feel the energy is stuck or where there is pain or tightness. Be aware of any areas of your body that feel unloved or neglected. After the body scan, answer the following questions:

Today my body is feeling _____ because I notice that _____.

Today my body needs _____, so I will_____.

Journal Questions:

What did I notice during the body scan? What did I learn?

Did it help me to plan my day, while taking the needs of my body into consideration?

Do I think this will be a helpful tool going forward? Why?

When You Need a Break

When you need a break from all the medical appointments and treatments, consider taking an art break by *coloring*. As a child, I used to love to color because it allowed me to escape my painful environment and provided me with moments of peace and contentment. These pockets of creative bliss were crucial to my well-being. Coloring is such a healing activity that I would like you to experience it as an adult.

Adult coloring is a great tool for people who don't consider themselves to be "creative" and for those who can benefit from a more contained creative process. A study published in the *Creativity Research Journal* (2017), called "Sharpen Your Pencils: Preliminary Evidence That Adult Coloring Reduces Depressive Symptoms and Anxiety" states, "Coloring participants showed significantly lower levels of depressive symptoms and anxiety after the intervention, but control participants did not. We conclude that daily coloring can improve some negative psychological outcomes and that it may provide an effective, inexpensive, and highly accessible self-help tool for nonclinical samples."

Coloring is also a great way to practice mindfulness. I know that when one is not feeling well, it is difficult to sit still and meditate, so another option is to take a *mindful* creative break and color. Adult coloring books are a great way of focusing on one thing at a time, which helps to calm the mind. While coloring, use all your senses to get you into a mindful state. For example, pay attention to the feel of the crayons and the repetitive movements of your hand, the scent of the wax, and the vibrant colors on the page. Just like meditation, coloring allows your brain to focus on the *present moment*, helping to alleviate free-floating anxiety. When I color, I notice that my breathing rate slows down and I connect to the feeling that I had as a kid while I was coloring, which is peace and contentment. We can all use some of that while going through treatment!

Note: When buying coloring books for yourself, consider books that have larger images that are easier to color, because sometimes chemotherapy affects vision or causes neuropathy, making it difficult to color tiny spaces.

Studies have shown that *mindful coloring* is a simple way to connect to our creativity. This slowing down and relaxing allows us to access the right brain, which is our creative center. In this section (and throughout the book), I have provided you with beautiful images for you to enjoy because I want you to experience all the wonderful benefits from such an easy and beneficial tool.

Activity: Coloring Book

Take this book to your doctor's office and treatment appointments to help you reduce anxiety. This mini coloring book is brought to you by the students of Eastlake High School, in Chula Vista, California (2018). All you need are some colored pencils or crayons. Enjoy!

Let your smile change the world, but don't let the world change your smile.
~ Connor Franta

STAND TALL.

Journal Questions:

How did coloring the pictures make me feel?

Was I able to experience mindfulness?

Can I use this as a tool when I am feeling anxious? Or frustrated?

When You Are Bedridden

Frida Kahlo, the famous Mexican painter, spent many months of her life in bed recovering from a painful accident and illnesses, but she did not let that stop her from creating. She painted self-portraits as an outlet to express what she was going through physically, mentally, and emotionally. She refused to be a victim of her circumstances. She used her creativity to give her "wings to fly." Instead of asking yourself *Why me?* —which is from a place of powerlessness—can you shift your perspective to one of *What can I do, even from bed?* The second question empowers you to shift to things that you can control.

Making art, even from your bed, keeps you focused on something that is pleasant, thus allowing you to forget about your problems and fears for a while. In a study about art therapy and art-making in the *Journal of Health Psychology* (2006), researchers Collie, Bottorff, and Long interviewed participants about the art-making process. The researchers reported of a participant, "Hannah made the point that art is something people can do even when illness has made it impossible to do other things, they may have been accustomed to doing to feel alive and whole."

If you are thinking, *I am too tired to be creative,* **think about this:** A study done at Albion College in Michigan about creative problem-solving showed that when the test subjects were fatigued, it improved their creative problem-solving abilities by 20 percent! Feeling tired while you are being creative allows you to be open to other channels for insight and problem-solving, which is empowering. Have fun with the following activity.

Activity: What Creative Activities Can I Do in Bed?

Can you do things, even if you are not feeling well that make you feel alive and whole?

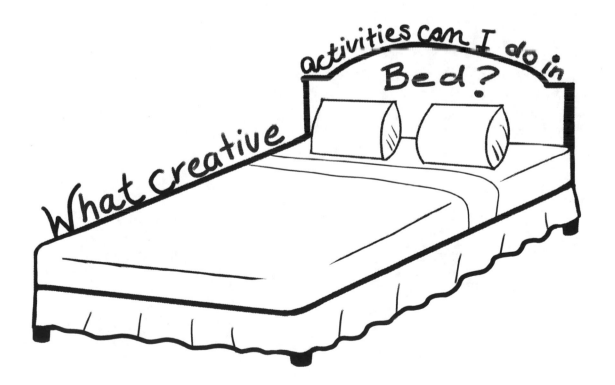

When You Don't Feel Attractive

Mirror, mirror on the wall...
It does not matter if I'm short or tall...
If I have skinny legs or my hips are wide...
It only matters who I am inside...
Blue eyes, brown eyes, black or green...
What makes me most beautiful cannot be seen...
When you look at me, don't judge me by my parts...
The most beautiful thing about me is my heart.

-Unknown

Cancer strips away everything that is superficial and unimportant, like trying to have the perfect hair and body. As you go through cancer treatment, you are going to have unwanted changes to your body. Part of your recovery will include accepting and loving these changes.

I think one of the hardest things for my clients is losing their hair. This would be a traumatic experience for anyone. The hardest part of losing your hair is that it is a visible reminder of cancer that you and everyone else can see. I found it helped my clients to be proactive to hair loss by choosing to cut their hair off on their terms.

Client Stories

One of my clients made losing her hair into a party. She went to the salon to have her head shaved with a group of loving and supportive friends and family, celebrating the event with music, cake, and balloons. She turned something that could have been traumatic into a beautiful and fun experience.

I had another client who wore a blue cosplay wig (cosplay is dressing up as a character from a movie, book, or video game) after she shaved her head. The first time I saw her walk into the room, she was wearing a blue long-haired wig, a short skirt, and sunglasses. She looked like a rock star and every man in the room turned to look at her!

Another client, who just became a grandmother for the first time, bought matching beanies (hats) for her and her granddaughter's bald heads.

It is hard to feel attractive when you do not feel well, therefore I encourage all my coaching clients to take the "Look Good, Feel Better" class. All of my clients who took the class raved about how wonderful it made them feel and look. The website states the following: "Look Good, Feel Better is a nonmedical brand-neutral public service program that teaches beauty techniques to people with cancer to help them manage the appearance-related side effects of cancer treatment. The program includes lessons on skin and nail care, cosmetics, wigs and turbans, accessories and styling, thus helping people with cancer to find some normalcy in a life that is by no means normal." Check their website (www.lookgoodfeelbetter.org) for local classes that are open to all women who are undergoing cancer treatment. They are well worth your time.

Making art has been shown to improve body image. In a study published in the *European Journal of Cancer Care*, Dr. Jack Lindh states, "Women who participated in an art therapy group that had been diagnosed with major stresses, due to breast cancer, showed significant improvements in the reduction of stress and improvement in their body image."

Activity: Rumi Poem

I love the message of the following Rumi poem:

> *I am not my hair,*
> *I am not my skin,*
> *I am the soul that lives within.*

I have shared this poem with clients who were adjusting to changes in their body to use as an affirmation that true beauty lies within. Enjoy coloring the following image of a woman holding the poem while thinking of what makes you feel attractive.

I am not my hair, I am not my skin,
I am the soul that lives within. Rumi

When you are going through the physical and psychological changes cancer brings, it helps to use your journal to explore or redefine your idea of what makes you feel attractive. It helps to focus on the inner qualities you possess that make you feel beautiful as a person.

Journal Questions:

What is my definition of an attractive or beautiful person? Has this changed since my diagnosis?

What things can I do to feel attractive internally and externally?

What does the Rumi poem mean to me? Do I have a favorite quote or poem that inspires true beauty?

When You Are Feeling Fatigued

In the *European Journal of Cancer Care* (January 27, 2018), a review of fifteen studies on the art-making process for people with a cancer diagnosis explored how art-making could help address their fatigue. The study states, "Art-making can be understood as an energy-restoring activity that has the potential to enhance the lives of people with a diagnosis of cancer."

This study confirmed what I have always experienced, that the creative or art-making process has an energizing effect that can help you when you are fatigued. Creative activities allow you to tap into reservoirs of energy that help you overcome fatigue and feel a sense of control over the side effects of treatment.

Answer the following questions to explore what creative things get your juices flowing with excitement.

Activity: Fighting Fatigue with Creativity

What creative activities get me excited about doing them?

What activities seem to give me more energy?

What activities can I plan on a weekly or daily basis to help me feel energized?

When You Want More Delight in Your Life

When you slow down and see, taste, smell, and touch what is in front of you every moment, you will find wonder and delight in the smallest experience.

—Hari Kaur Khala, *A Woman's Book of Meditation*

Sometimes when we are not feeling well, we avoid excessive sensory stimuli. We limit going out in public because it increases our chances of getting sick when our immune system is low. We avoid going out to eat at our favorite restaurant because the spicy food might upset our stomach. We avoid being out in nature end enjoying the warmth of the sun because we have to limit sun exposure due to chemotherapy. Reducing your sensory exposure also results in the deprivation of those soothing and pleasant things that might help you to feel better. While going through this difficult time, I want you to remember that sensory experiences can nurture and lift your spirits.

Creative expression can facilitate the joyful connection to your senses and body. It can help you to feel *whole* because creating art is a multi-sensory experience. By connecting to enjoyable sensory experiences through the art-making process, you contribute to your sense of well-being.

While painting, you use your vision, to see the colors across the canvas. Your hand holds the brush and touches the canvas as you move your body. There is the scent of oil or acrylic paints. You may hear the brush being stroked across the canvas. The multisensory experience of making art has a soothing and integrative component that other forms of healing do not have. The process of creating allows you to forget about your pain and suffering for a moment and experience this sense of oneness, putting your body in the relax-and-renew healing state.

You can actively choose sensory experiences that will help you feel better, self-soothe, and self-comfort. For example, a soft sweater, and luxurious bed linens can all promote comfort thru the sense of *touch*. Aromatherapy, or the scent of freshly cut flowers, can delight your sense of *smell*. The *sound* of people laughing can raise your spirits and the sounds of nature can calm you down. Nothing *tastes* better than your favorite comfort foods when you are feeling down. In the next activity, we are going to explore what delights us so we can do more of it!

Activity: Sensory Delight

What delights my sense of taste?

What delights my sense of touch?

What delights my sense of smell?

What sounds do I find delightful?

What delights me visually?

Activity: Little Pleasures

Increasing your delight is not hard to do because most of the time it involves little things that bring you happiness and a sense of well-being. Small things that provide you comfort can be clean sheets on your bed, fresh strawberries with your breakfast, or your favorite cup of tea with honey.

Small things can also provide emotional comfort, like hanging out with your best friend and watching your favorite movie. Think of little things that you can do throughout the day that bring you pleasure in the following activity, then enjoy coloring the drawing.

I have included the following drawing for your coloring pleasure.

CHAPTER 8

Creative Prescription 6: Cultivate a Spiritual Practice

If we cannot be happy in spite of our difficulties, what good is our spiritual practice?

—Maha Ghosananda, Buddhist monk

Spiritual Practice and Cancer

A cancer diagnosis can prompt you to reevaluate everything in your life, including your spiritual beliefs. As a cancer coach, I work with women from many different religious practices and beliefs. One thing is true for all of them: Women who have strong religious or spiritual practices did much better mentally and emotionally while going through their cancer treatment. They could lean on their faith and religious community to give them strength.

A meta-analysis (analysis of multiple studies) by Heather S.L. Jim, PhD, in *Cancer* (2015), showed that participants who had religious or spiritual beliefs in a higher power reported "A stronger ability to cope with cancer." In addition, it improved "physical recovery and quality of life." It did not matter what belief system they used; it was the sense of spiritual connection that was important.

If you do not have a spiritual or religious practice, it's not too late to start one! If you do not believe in a higher power, that's okay. You can use rituals that promote healing and restore a sense of hope and wholeness.

Note: I may have a spiritual practice that differs from what you believe in. This section is meant to be inclusive of all spiritual and religious beliefs, so if you see a word that is not what you use, please insert the word that you are comfortable with.

Annette Tello, M.S.

Whether you decide to redefine your beliefs or strengthen them, making spiritual sense of your cancer diagnosis is important to your sense of well-being. You may have to rethink what now gives your life spiritual quality and meaning. Many of my clients see cancer as a sacred doorway to spiritual growth. To explore your beliefs, answer the following questions.

Journal Questions:

How have my beliefs changed since my diagnosis?

How can my beliefs support me during my treatment and recovery?

In what ways can I deepen my spiritual practice?

Exploring Creativity as a Spiritual Practice

At its core, art is the expression of the Spirit, the Divine Creator. No matter what your spiritual beliefs are, art heals via this creative life force.

—Mary Rockwood Lane

Throughout human history, and in most cultures of the world, art has been a form of spiritual expression. Many artists, writers, and musicians have stated that creating was a spiritual practice and they were divinely guided while creating. You can use art-making as a doorway to connect to your spiritual wisdom. Creating art can lift your spirits and promote your soul's wellness. Exploring creative pathways to spiritual fulfillment can help you find meaning during your cancer treatment and recovery.

In 2017, the Intentional Creativity Foundation conducted a study within their community. The study found:

89% - included creativity as a part of their spiritual practice

89% - feel a sense of connection with the divine [while making art]

Your creative practice can be a devotional practice, allowing you to worship on paper and canvas. In my community, an art studio has a class on Sunday called "art church." This class creates a sacred space where people can create art within a like-minded community.

> *I see my art as a gift from God to share with others.*
> —Donna Ogle, journal artist

On occasion, I teach a workshop that allows the participants to "paint their prayers" (for information, visit www.annettetello.com). It is a workshop for making art from your "inner church." Creating *spiritual* art can be very fulfilling because it is an expression of your soul, helping you feel connected to the divine. In the following section, you will have a chance to deepen your spiritual connection through the *Creative Prescriptions* process.

Creative Prescriptions Tools and Activities

This section covers *Creative Prescriptions* tools, journal questions, and activities to help you explore and deepen your spiritual practice through the creative process. Select the topic(s) you need in this moment to create your own prescription.

When You Need Help from a Higher Power

> *A healthy spiritual life generates positive emotion, which reduces stress and distress, which boost immune cell system, which fights cancer using the killer cells and the T cells.*
>
> —Francisco Contreras, MD

When you need help from a higher power, nothing beats the power of prayers. Prayers give us the courage and strength to go through treatment because we have faith that everything will be all right.

On dictionary.com, prayer is defined as:

1. A solemn request for help or expression of thanks addressed to God or an object of worship
2. An earnest hope or wish

Prayers do not have to be a formal request to benefit you. As stated in the definition, they can be an earnest wish; they can also be an affirmation. Prayer has many positive effects on the body, such as the ability to improve your immune system and promote healing. Studies show that prayers initiate the relaxation response, which releases oxytocin, a feel-good hormone.

It is also comforting to know that others are praying for us. Cardiologist Randolf Byrd did a study with two groups of cardiac patients. One group was prayed for; one was not. Those who were prayed for had fewer complications and higher survival rates than the non-prayer group.

Prayer can generate an energy field around a person who is being prayed for. We are a family with a lot of praying power, so when my cousin was diagnosed with lung cancer, I told him I was praying for him. He said, "I know. I can physically feel that I am being prayed for; I feel surrounded by love." He felt the healing power of prayer on a physical, emotional, and spiritual level.

Client Story

One of my clients had a severe reaction to her first round of chemotherapy. She ended up in the hospital in critical condition. Her mother called the members of her church and asked them to pray for her. Not only did she get better; the scans done once she stabilized showed the cancer tumor was no longer visible on any of the scans. Now that is the power of prayer!

If you have never experienced the healing energy of prayer, consider attending a healing prayer service that many churches offer for those who need extra support while going through illness. Use the power of prayer for yourself by asking family, friends, coworkers, and neighbors to pray for you. Hospitals usually have a chaplain on staff who will pray with you. There are also religious organizations that take prayer requests. Even Facebook friends will pray for you if you request it.

Activity: Visual Prayer

I feel passionate about visual prayer because it has helped me deepen my relationship with God, heal, and continues to bring beauty to my life.
—Valerie Sjodin, artist

You can make any creative activity a prayer/affirmation by sending an intention to serve your highest good. In the following activity, you will create a visual prayer by adding your favorite prayer to the image, then color it in. Feel free to place the image on your wall to remind you of the power of prayer.

When You Worry Too Much

It is so hard not to worry when you are waiting for the results of a lab test or scan. I am guilty of worrying to the point of obsessing, so I have learned to reframe my thoughts. I love this quote from *A Woman's Book of Meditation*. This is just one example of reframing your thoughts about worry.

> *Worry is misplaced prayer. If you find yourself worrying too much, try to reframe your worrisome thoughts into a form of prayer or affirmation. This can help shift negative thought patterns to positive and healing thoughts which helps reduce stress.*
> —Hari Kaur Khalsa, *A Woman's Book of Meditation*

If you are worried about the effectiveness of your chemotherapy, try to change your worry to a prayer/affirmation. For example, "I trust that my chemotherapy will be one hundred percent effective" or, "I pray that the chemotherapy is one hundred percent effective in eradicating the cancer." "Eradicate" is from the Latin word *eradicare*, meaning "to root out." These small shifts in the way you think about your treatment go a long way in reducing stress and giving you peace of mind.

Activity: Reframing Worry

Reframe a thought that is worrying you, change it into a prayer or affirmation and add it to the image on the following page. Then enjoy coloring the image.

Kristen Neff, researcher and author of the book *Self-Compassion*, uses the following mantra for worry:

> *May I be free of worry*
> *May I be well*
> *May I feel safe and at ease*
> *May I be at peace*

Sometimes the burden feels too hard to handle, so it is a relief that you can surrender your worries to a higher source. A great prayer to alleviate worry is the Serenity Prayer, written by Reinhold Niebuhr.

Activity: Serenity Prayer

Enjoy coloring the following image while repeating the prayer.

God, grant me the

Serenity to accept the things I cannot change,

Courage to change the things I can, and the

Wisdom to know the difference.

Reinhold Niebuhr

When You Need Hope

> *Spiritual experiences such as hope and transcendence may be realized through the creative process.*
> —Cathy A. Malchiodi, *The Art Therapy Sourcebook*

Religious and spiritual beliefs give people faith and hope, which is crucial for recovering from cancer. Faith gives us the ability to believe deeply in our souls that everything will be okay. When one has faith, one has hope. Hope is a force that will strengthen your will to live. Whether you call it your Creator, God, or Universal love, the faith in something greater than ourselves gives us a great sense of hope when we are going through difficult times.

Studies have shown that doctors who fill their patients with hope and encouragement have much higher success rates with patients than those who have doctors who do not. The following activity will help you strengthen the feelings of hope in your life.

Activity: Hope Collage

Supplies: scissors, glue stick, markers, and a collection of your favorite prayers, verses from spiritual text, quotes, and images that create a sense of hope for you.

While selecting images, ask yourself, What helps me feel hopeful during difficult times?

Cut and arrange the items in a sense that is pleasing to you and glue them on the following blank page. Look at your "hope collage" whenever you need an extra boost of hope.

What helps me feel hopeful during difficult times?

When You Need Spiritual Comfort

God gives us many tools for healing and comfort, such as spending time in sacred space; this could be a church, a synagogue, or maybe in a quiet garden. Making art can provide a path to spiritual strength and comfort. When I am going through a difficult period in my life or a crisis, I know that my faith and my creativity can comfort me.

> *For me, art journaling is inextricably intertwined with my faith. Art feeds my faith and faith feeds my art.*
>
> —Tracy Woodsford,
> author of *Hands on Bible Creativity*

Client Story

One of my coaching clients wanted to strengthen her faith. She set a goal of having a daily spiritual practice of coloring in a religious coloring book that had images and passages from the Bible. While coloring she would contemplate the Bible verse. After completing a picture, she would put it up on her bedroom wall. She stated that this activity provided her with spiritual comfort and strength when she was alone.

Activity: Spiritual Comfort Angel

When you are not feeling well, it is good to know what gives you spiritual comfort and do those things consciously. Fill in the four boxes around the following "angel of comfort" with four things that bring you spiritual comfort. Then enjoy coloring the image.

Things that bring me spiritual comfort:

When You Want to Communicate with the Divine

In addition to praying, writing letters is a way for you to honestly express what is in your heart and soul. In the following activity, you will write a letter to God, then you will write what you feel God would say to you in response. Do this in your private journal or use loose sheets of lined paper. If you do not feel comfortable doing this, the letter can be to your guardian angel, a spiritual guide, a loved one, or your highest self. I love to do this when I am going through a rough time and need emotional support; it can be a very magical and healing experience!

Activity: Letter to the Divine

On two separate sheets of writing paper, complete the following activities:

Letter to the Divine

Dear God,

(Response to your letter)

Dear beloved,

Devotional Journaling

> *As I create and listen, I will be led.*
> —Julia Cameron, *The Artist's Way*

A devotional journal is another way to communicate with the Divine. Devotional journaling slows me down so I can be open and receptive to messages from Spirit. In Janet Connor's book *Writing Down Your Soul*, she uses her daily journaling practice to meditate and communicate with her Creator. The following activity will help you get started on your devotional journal.

Activity: My Devotional Journal

Buy a personal journal that you will use for Divine guidance. Here are some questions to get you started:

What am I yearning for in my relationship with God?

What practices help me feel connected to a higher power?

What do I need to be spiritually healthy?

What recharges my soul?

Am I living a life that is aligned with my soul and my Creator?

How do my thoughts about my illness affect my faith?

When You "Should" Be Meditating but You're Not

Learning to inhabit the stillness is our most powerful tool for dealing with chaos. Spending a few minutes each day alone with Spirit, we then go back into the world with a more open heart, expanded mind, and calmer nervous system.

—Marianne Williamson, author of A Return to Love

As women, we need downtime and sacred solitude to hear our own thoughts, to become aware of our own feelings and needs. Prayer is a two-way street, after praying, take some time to be still, in quiet contemplation/meditation, and listen to the messages from Spirit.

Why Meditate?

Common side effects of daily meditation are increased energy and feelings of contentedness and inner happiness.

—Light Watkins

Studies show that meditation is a proven way to reduce stress, master your emotional reactions, calm your mind, and enhance happiness. What could be better than that? If this were in a pill form, everyone would take it.

Meditation works by deactivating the brain's default mode, which can keep you stuck in negative thought and behavior patterns. Once the default setting is deactivated, your mind calms down and opens up to new insights. When you are not stuck in worry and negative thoughts, you have the ability to tap into the joy that is always part of your connection with the Divine. Meditating can help you gain peace of mind, which helps to reduce anxiety and physical tension. This allows your body to activate self-healing. It also helps you to become less reactive to stressful situations, which is helpful during cancer treatment.

> *Meditation rewires us for happiness.*
> —Dr. Richard Davidson

Does meditating lead to survivorship? Studies show that meditating does improve the quality of life for cancer survivors. In Ian Gawler's book *You Can Conquer Cancer,* he wrote how meditation was instrumental in helping him heal from stage IV cancer. He now teaches other cancer patients how to meditate and states that his students "attribute meditation as a factor in their survival [of cancer]."

So why are you not meditating? Some women give up on meditation because it is too difficult to make their minds go blank or empty. Meditation has been misunderstood. *Meditation is not about stopping your thoughts;* it is about being aware of them and redirecting your focus back to an object or your breath/body.

Some women do not meditate because they feel it is a spiritual practice that is not part of their own religious practice. It is true that meditation is a spiritual practice for various religions. However, just as prayer is used across all major religions, meditation is a practice that can be used by different faiths to deepen spiritual connection. So please do not let the word *meditation* turn you off to using this amazing tool for healing in your life! If you feel more comfortable, use the phrase "my quiet time."

Different Types of Meditation

Let's dive a little deeper into the different types of meditation so you can find one that you will feel comfortable doing. There are three types of meditation, and within each type, there are different ways of doing it:

Concentrative Meditation

This is a practice where you focus on an image, sound, a repeated prayer (such as praying the rosary), or a simple mantra, such as "Om" or "Peace."

Mindfulness Meditation

One example of this type of meditation is the mindfulness-based stress reduction program developed by Jon Kabat-Zinn, which integrates Eastern meditation with Western medicine and science. This program is offered in many medical centers, to help people manage anxiety, stress, and pain. This is a good highly-researched nonreligious option that focuses on the scientific benefits of meditation.

Expressive Meditation

This is the oldest type of meditation, and it usually involves expression and movement, such as dancing, and creating art. This is the meditation we will focus on in this section because when you are not feeling well, it can be hard to sit still and meditate, but you can still get the benefits of meditation through art-making. People who express themselves through the visual arts call this *meditative art* or *creative meditation.*

> *Creative meditation offers an opportunity to be less controlling and much more playful both in your artwork and in your daily life.*
> —Rebecca Schweiger, *Release Your Creativity*

In meditative art, the focus is the artist's inner state. When you are deeply engaged with your art-making process, it allows you to be in the state of "flow," which is like meditation. When you are in this state, you benefit from the same healing benefits described in the research done on meditation.

Anecdote

There was a spiritual teacher who was teaching a class on the benefits of meditation. In the front of the room was an older woman who would nod in agreement as he made his points. After the class, he approached the woman and said, "I see you are familiar with the benefits of meditation." The woman nodded and said, "Well, I do crochet, you know."

There are many good books and online videos on how to do concentrative and mindfulness meditation. In the next section, we will experience *expressive meditation* through the art of making a mandala.

Mandala Meditation

> *Self-created mandalas are reflections of your inner self and are*
> *symbolic of your potential for change and transformation.*
> —Cathy Malchiodi, *The Soul's Palette*

Mandalas help us to experience the benefits of meditation without having to sit still for long periods of time. This is a great option for those of you who have been unsuccessful with meditation or are not feeling well. *Mandala* means circle in Sanskrit. In many religions, the circle is seen as a container for the *sacred*. It is an ancient symbol for wholeness. The circle is used to bring forth images that can be used for healing and transformation. I like to draw mandalas because they are relaxing, yet they can also be profound.

Activity: Open-Eyed Mandala Meditation

In the following activity, we are doing an open-eyed meditation, which means you do not have to close your eyes and sit still to do it. To make it a meditative experience, create a space that is free of distraction. Be mindful of being present in your body, and let your mind focus on the image as you color. You can light a candle and play relaxing or spiritual music while coloring the following Mandala:

When You Need to Forgive

Forgiveness is giving up the hope that the past could have been any different. It's accepting the past for what it was, and using this moment and this time to help yourself move forward.

—Oprah Winfrey

In his book *Cancer: 50 Essential Things to Do*, Greg Anderson credits *forgiving* his abusive father as pivotal in healing his stage IV lung cancer. Greg Anderson was diagnosed with metastatic lung cancer in 1984, with his doctor only giving him thirty days to live. He fully recovered, and he is the author of many inspirational books for cancer patients.

Activity: Forgiveness Practice

Greg Anderson has a forgiveness practice that I love. He recommends that each day you choose one person to forgive and say the following:

"[person's name], I totally and completely forgive you.

I release you to the care of God. I affirm your highest good."

Journal Questions:

Sometimes we have to forgive ourselves. What do you need to forgive yourself for, in order to feel at ease?

Have I found forgiveness difficult? Why?

Annette Tello, M.S.

Where in my life is my cancer calling me to be more forgiving?

Who are the people I need to forgive?

CHAPTER 9

After Treatment

The artwork that matters most—the canvas of your life—is a combination of your precious experiences and memories, your joys and your sorrows, the actions you take to consciously create a life that you love with all of your heart.

—Rebecca Schweiger, *Release Your Creativity*

Completing treatment is a time to rejoice and celebrate! However, even though you are done with treatment you may not be done with the healing process, and therefore still need support. Many women have been so busy with treatment that they haven't had the chance to process all the changes in their life. They know they are not the same person, but they don't quite know who they are.

If you still need support don't be afraid to say so. Feel free to use this book throughout the peaks and valleys of your life. If you need help adjusting to the changes that have occurred within yourself, your body, and your relationships, seek the assistance of a therapist or social worker.

Going Forward, How Do I Want to Feel?

Use creativity to weave a new life for yourself.

I encourage you to take some time to find out what your new "normal" is and what is important to you now. Cancer changes your priorities, so take this opportunity to think about what you *really* want going forward in your life!

In her book *The Desire Map,* Danielle La Porte talks about setting your goals for the different areas of your life based on *how you want to feel after you achieved the goals.* Most goals are set through the logical mind, such as "I want a better-paying job" or "I want to lose ten pounds." In La Porte's book, a goal or intention is determined by how we want to *feel* in our new job or how we want to *feel* when we are ten pounds lighter.

To do this, it's important for you to be clear on what kinds of experiences can effect/determine how you want to *feel*. Once you are clear about how you want to *feel*, it is easier to make micro (small) decisions throughout the day that are in alignment with that intention. The following story is how a coaching client successfully applied this to help her make positive lifestyle changes.

Client Story

"Many people think I have amazing willpower to be able to choose a salad over an incredible juicy gourmet hamburger. However, it's actually not willpower at all. I know that if I eat the hamburger, I will feel heavy and tired afterward. If I eat the salad with protein, it will give me the energy that I need for the rest of the day. It helps that I am in tune with my body and know how certain foods make me feel, so it's easy to make these micro-decisions (hamburger or salad?) when I set the goal of wanting to feel healthy and energized by the choices I make. This made it easy for me to lose weight while increasing my energy level."

Now that you have completed treatment, set your goals/intentions on how you want to *feel* going forward in your life and begin making the small decisions that increase those feelings throughout your day. You can do this in every area of your life.

Activity: How Do I Want to Feel?

Now that you have completed treatment, how do you want to *feel* going forward? Take some time to think about what changes you can make in your life to increase those feelings.

Take some time to think about what changes you can make in your life to increase how you want to feel. Close your eyes and picture yourself in the future, what are you doing? What is your vision of yourself? Does it feel right in body, mind and soul? Write about what kind of life you want going forward in your journal. Then set your goals to achieve your dreams.

Benefits of Having a Cancer Coach

After completing treatment many survivors want to make significant life style changes to reduce the risk of reoccurrence. Sometimes they can implement healthier habits for themselves but are not able to maintain the long-term changes they want to see in their lives. If you need support in making health and life changes, consider working with a cancer coach. They understand what you have been through and what challenges you face as a cancer survivor. A cancer coach is a partner who will help you develop and implement an action plan to live your best life.

In a study, published in *The International Journal of Interdisciplinary Social Sciences* in December 2009, 30 cancer survivors participated in a wellness coaching program over a three-month period. **The results of coaching showed a decrease in depression and anxiety, better motivation, increased physical activity, and a healthier diet.**

Cancer coaches help clients to:

Work on strategies to prevent re-occurrence by identifying risk factors and addressing those factors. This may include nutrition, environment, lifestyle, emotional and physical health.

Set attainable goals, like increasing energy, managing weight, improving physical fitness, and improving memory and focus.

Be accountable to their goals with firm, non-judgmental support.

Overcome obstacles that are keeping them from achieving their goals.

Discover their life purpose and create a new path to living it.

I combine holistic cancer coaching and life coaching in my *Cancer to Wellness Program*. I will help you move forward in your life as a stronger, wiser, more emotionally-healthy, and creative version of yourself. People expect you to be different after a cancer diagnosis, so take this opportunity to make the changes you have been wanting to make!

Contact me if you are looking for a coach who is highly-experienced, creative, compassionate, and has a holistic approach to healing.

Are you ready to embark upon your wellness journey? I am here for you, at www.annettetello.com.

In Conclusion

I hope this book has provided you with many wonderful creative coping tools that you will continue using throughout your life. But most of all, I hope you keep creating!

If you have enjoyed this book please leave a good review on Amazon.com, and share it with other women going through cancer.

You are welcome to join our online Facebook community and share your artwork in a group that is respectful and supportive. Our page is Fb.me/creativeprescriptions.

Please check out my website www.annettetello.com if you would like to contact me, attend a workshop, or for additional information. **Join my email list for bonus material!**

> *She brings a sense of fun and play into a time of crisis, anger, anxiety, and depression. Her goal is to help you conquer your inner critic and other fears that keep you from trusting your creative voice and its healing benefits. Let her guide you to discover a new way of viewing yourself by experiencing the benefits of creative expression.*
> —*Creative Prescriptions* workshop participant

Now go out and weave a happy, healthy, creative life for yourself!

About Author

Annette Tello, M.S., has twenty-five years of experience in rehabilitation counseling and coaching. Creative expression through art-making was a critical tool in her own healing, and it inspired her to write this book. She has a wealth of experience designing and facilitating workshops, classes, and support groups. By sharing her experience as a coach and artist, she hopes to inspire others to use creativity as a doorway to a more mindful, healthier, and joy-filled life. She lives in San Diego with the love of her life, Jim, and their pets.

Printed in the United States
By Bookmasters